Pattern of the
Land

Pattern of the *Land*

The Search for Home
in an Altered Landscape

EILEEN APPERSON

iUniverse

PATTERN OF THE LAND
The Search for Home in an Altered Landscape

Versions of essays taken from this book have been published in:
Platte Valley Review
San Joaquin Review
Writing It Real

Passages from this book are featured in the film:
The Phantom Lake: Between Farming and Nature

Tulare Lake Basin maps courtesy of the Sequoia Genealogical Society

iUniverse books may be ordered through booksellers or by contacting:

iUniverse
1663 Liberty Drive
Bloomington, IN 47403
www.iuniverse.com
1-800-Authors (1-800-288-4677)

ISBN: 978-1-4697-8221-8 (sc)
ISBN: 978-1-4697-8222-5 (e)

Print information available on the last page.

iUniverse rev. date: 06/02/2017

To Mom and Dad,
with love and gratitude

1

If you don't know where you are, you don't know who you are.

—Wendell Berry

IN THE EARLY morning hours I would sooth myself into the oak rocking chair that once belonged to my grandfather, my hungry infant daughter in my arms. These were my favorite experiences of being a new mother, a sense of timelessness. It was then that I began the story telling as, I have been told, was done for me. I whispered to her for the first time family stories and dreams I wished for her future. *Someday you will rock your own baby in this chair,* I let her know. *And you will be willful like the women in our family . . . Let me tell you about Aunt Lorraine, whom you are named after . . .*

Once her feeding was over, as I rocked her back to sleep, she would look past me, somewhere into the quiet over my shoulder, and smile. Sleepily wondering who she saw, I drifted, once dreaming my grandparents were standing behind us, their stories I had recounted beckoning them. Peering over us, they had come to see their great-grandchild and argue over whose looks she favored; the almond-shaped eyes of the Beaver family and the Peck's auburn hair, they must have surmised.

My grandmother, Genevieve, once said she would give anything to just be able to rock one of her babies again. I felt her there with me, child in arms, that morning. I dreamed of infant and spirits communicating with one another in a language only they could comprehend. What was it my daughter was asking them with her coos, her eyes growing brighter, and then faintly smiling as she closed them back to sleep?

If only I were so privileged into this conversation. What would it be that I would ask them? I already knew so much of their lives, mostly through stories which my parents told me. Most people would want to know names, dates and places, the missing pieces among the family story. I know the names and dates, and especially the place, growing up very near where my grandparents Carl and Genevieve also grew up 80 years prior. The landscape is now vastly different from what they saw. What I long for is to know what they felt about the land they worked, what they saw of nature, what was their sense of home and belonging. I may not like their answers. They may have viewed this place as a challenge to conquer and control, to use and make profitable. As with so many transplanted people, home may have always remained a family homestead in Missouri or Illinois, not this virgin landscape.

And even though I too was raised on a farm, aware of the need for profit, I am more interested in what lay before, having difficulty finding a sense of place amid an altered landscape. Although I stand in an orchard in awe of what is the most extensive and powerful agricultural region in the world, I long to connect to a landscape gone for over a century. Besides their stories, there are boxes of mementos and photographs and china cabinets filled with heirlooms to connect me to these people, but living in the place where they once lived gives me another, more visceral connection, the landscape.

It is a test to imagine a terrain that no longer exists. We are left with only fragments from first observers. California's San Joaquin Valley was described as both an Eden, a green promised land, and a hell, scorched and barren. The account depended on the visitor's locale, time of year, and, most importantly, intent for the land.

As a child, my own feelings about this place brought the same irresolution. What I needed was a place where I felt at home. The journey continued to be a long one. I have always sensed deep connections to landscape and the one I knew best was a hazy mixture of angular fields, barbed wire, and housing tracts enveloping old, stoic farmhouses. The landscape I was longing for was beneath all this, showing through in the very few patches of wilderness along the narrow river winding its way through the valley.

"Tell me the landscape in which you live, and I will tell you who you are," wrote Jose Ortega y Gassett, and I believe nothing is truer. Traveling in another country once, I was advised to say that I was a Californian rather than an American, for Americans are not always liked, a response similarly made by the state's first settlers. These pioneers of Mexican descent referred to themselves only as Californios. Their attachment to the land defined themselves more than their nationality. The response I received from Londoners to Frankfurters was emphatic and so consistent that it has strengthened the way I began to see myself, as they saw me. I am of California, and more so a place foreigners would not know if I told them. I am of the San Joaquin Valley, in a region where the Kings River flows from the Sierra in the direction of what once was Tulare Lake, passing nearby the farm I grew up on, at the edge of Kingsburg, to land which my great-grandparents first settled in Lemoore. It is a place that has continued to give something new to each generation and which its people so eagerly accept and use. The evolution of the landscape that has taken place in the San Joaquin Valley is possibly no different than other landscapes that have changed over time, but it has happened before the weathered faces of my family who have called this place home, from my great-grandparents who were among the first white settlers, to my father who returned to the land because he saw its beauty, however scarred, and resisted its next alteration.

To really know a place is to know the landscape and so in trying to know my home I began with what I knew best, my family. Unlike most of the valley's inhabitants who arrived during the Depression and Dust Bowl era and recent comers finding work in the fields and growing industries, my father's family moved into a frontier. They turned fields for the first time, diverted waters into land that had only seen it from the sky, and built the first homes and communities. It has taken a long time to realize that they have become my connection to the land.

MY GRANDMOTHER, GENEVIEVE Beaver Apperson, made a final trip home to the San Joaquin Valley from Los Angeles at age 90. My parents and I took her to see the town of her youth, in the neighboring county of our newly transplanted home. It was the first time she had been back to Lemoore in almost seventy years. She wept at the gravesites of her parents, siblings, and childhood friends, but her nervous laughter grew as we pulled up in front of the old Mooney house, now a museum. "That," she said pointing out the car window with a strong, steady finger, "is where I met your grandfather. There, at that wrought iron gate."

Twenty years later I found myself back at that same spot remembering my grandmother's laughter and tears, which always seemed to coincide. Walking through the newly painted white gate, I was searching for a familial connection, a history my grandmother did not leave me in the boxes of letters and photos she saved. The museum might have other documents, I thought, which would tie these people, my family, to the land. What I really wanted was personal accounts, like those I researched in historical records. I needed to know how they saw this nearly untouched landscape and worked the land into a home, beginning the evolution into the valley I know today. Did my great-grandparents value the land or what they could make the land become for them? Did they see its beauty amid their toil? At what point did this become our family's home?

A frail-looking woman met me at the door of the Mooney Museum. She welcomed me with apologies for being late while hurriedly moving from parlor to kitchen flipping on lights in the rooms and display cases. When I mentioned it wasn't necessary, that I was only looking for documents containing information about my great-grandparents' farm, she waved her hand and head in unison. She had to tell me the story of the Yokuts, emergence of farming, and rail expansion. And she continued to do so with a passion that only someone who had a history and love for the land could. Ten minutes into her lesson, I interrupted to ask how long her family had lived in the region. She blinked and said, "Oh, I just moved here three years ago." Her response took me aback and further complicated my desire for a connection to this place. What was it I was looking for if this woman, a stranger to this place, could sense kindred to her new home, and I, one with seemingly strong roots to a place, was conflicted? As I was contemplating my own purpose for my search, half listening to this woman's accounts of 1880's farm-life, she opened a trunk, pulled out a large quilt and said, "This may be of interest to you." She unfolded it before me, spreading it across the parlor floor.

It was a signature quilt made by Lemoore's 214 citizens. The quilt, partly resembling a wedding-band motif, has crimson circles atop a white background. Between each of these circles leaf-shaped appliques extend and unite the pattern. No doubt inspired by traditional styles, its design is unique. Scattered across the quilt neighbors signed their names in red ink that was then stitched over in tough, red thread. The similarly crimson backing held its color while the white had turned an ecru and was fraying in places. The quilt was completed in 1886 when the town was just forming and mirrors the well-planned pattern of the valley's surface at the hands of people such as my family. Schools and churches were rising and commerce growing. The railroad had just gone through; horse-drawn plows tilled and cultivated the expanse of outlying grasslands extending the angular lines of the rails, while canals spread out from the winding river. My great-grandparents' names are next to each other at one worn edge of the design: Mrs. Kate Beaver and Mr. J. W. Beaver. I knew James and Kate settled here in 1878, but this quilt tied them to a place, a belonging to a growing community, the well-plotted design a metaphor for the relationships between people and land, family and place. Its once virginal white foundation is worn with time and use, some of the residents' names faded more than others. This was a pivotal moment in my need to know how my family connected with their new home, my home, and sense of belonging.

What I have also found is my own strengthening attachment to my home as I look for the beauty which does remain in the farmland as well as in scant stretches as the Kings River winds its way, not only through the valley but through the places of my family's history.

2

The air is very clear this day—on the one side the Coast Range loomed up, barren and desolate, its scorched sides furrowed into canyons, every one of which was marvelously distinct; on the other side the distant Sierra, its cool snows glistening in the sun and mocking us on our scorching trail.

—William Brewer,
Up and Down California in 1860-64

WHILE ROAMING THROUGH the Westward Expansion Museum in St. Louis I came upon a topographical map of the continental United States as big and impressive as the grizzly bear which stood near it. My eyes went directly toward the San Joaquin Valley, what I have always considered the most distinct feature on the map, no matter its size. But then, perhaps, it is natural when looking at a map to first find the place you are from, comforting to see familiar land formations when away from home. I was contemplating these two notions when a small boy next to me approached the map. Standing on tiptoes, he reached his hand high as his extended finger rubbed up and down the smooth valley. He turned to his mother, who replied, "That is California."

More distinct than the wide expanse of the Rocky Mountains or Midwest Plains, the San Joaquin Valley does grab the viewer's eye, pulling it west to the long, thin vale. It is deeply carved and ceremoniously surrounded by equally defined mountain peaks; the impressive Sierra Nevada on its east, and completing the cradle, the Coast Range mountains to the west. According to the Yokut Indians of this region this is how these ranges were formed:

> Once there was a time when there was nothing in the world but water. About the place where Tulare Lake is now, there was a pole standing far up out of the water, and on this pole perched a hawk and a crow. First one of them would sit on the pole a while, then the other would knock him off and sit on it himself. Thus they sat on top of the pole above the waters for many ages. At length they wearied of the lonesomeness, and they created the birds which prey on fish such as the kingfisher, eagle, pelican, and others. Among them was a very small duck, which dived down to the bottom of the water, picked its beak full of mud, came up, died, and lay floating on the water. The hawk and crow then fell to work and gathered from the duck's beak the earth which it had brought up, and commenced making the mountains. They began at the place now known as Ta-hi-cha-pa Pass, and the hawk made the east range, while the crow made the west one. Little by little, as they dropped in the earth, these mountains

grew athwart the face of the waters, pushing north. It was a work of many years, but finally they met together at Mount Shasta, and their labors were ended. But, behold, when they compared their mountains, it was found that the crow's was a great deal larger. Then the hawk said to the crow, 'How did this happen, you rascal? I warrant you have been stealing some of the earth from my bill, and that is why the mountains are the biggest.' It was a fact and the crow laughed in his claws. Then the hawk went and got some Indian tobacco and chewed it, and it made him exceedingly wise. So he took hold of the mountains and turned them around in a circle, putting his range in place of the crow's; and that is why the Sierra Nevada is larger than the Coast Range.

Geologists will tell you that 140 million years before people and crops, nature began shaping the valley. At this time, the Jurassic period, there was no valley, no Sierra, no region we call California. The soil evolved from sedimentary sea-bottom to finally some of the richest earth in the world. In time the western edge of this sea warped itself into the life-giving Sierra. Run-off from its deep snowpack brought a mixture of minerals which were trapped under the valley's impervious clay lens creating subterranean waters which foreshadowed eventual settlement patterns across the valley floor.

From the river's entrance into the southern end of the valley, some 60 miles from its destination, the Kings meandered southwest through a varying landscape. These areas changed from riparian forest to savanna to marsh, moving east to west from the base of the Kings River's descent from the Sierra to the watery lands of Tulare Lake. The water of the river gave to the landscape its most obvious landmarks by nurturing the mixture of trees which lined the banks and asymmetrically tapered off into the level prairie. A tangle of deciduous oaks, Arizona and Oregon ash, California sycamore, willow, cottonwood, and walnut grew thick among wild berries, tules, and an assortment of native bunchgrasses to form a verdant maze in an otherwise arid land. A sanctuary was born as beavers, otters, and mink harbored the waters and blue herons and cranes glided down its bending flow. The river and its trees wound through the valley floor's prairie region until their end at the marsh of the lake near the west side of the valley.

At peak times the thriving lake consumed nearly 700 square miles of valley floor during run-off. This gave the lake the distinction of being the largest fresh-water lake west of the Mississippi during wet months. When water was low islands emerged in the shallow lake giving rest to wildlife who visited. Fish abounded in its waters. White sturgeon, Chinook salmon, and steelhead were able to spawn in the high water levels. Like the river, the lake itself was a biome of species, diverse and plentiful. Tule reeds grew straight toward the cloudless skies of summer and through the low-lying fog of winter to protect and nourish all the lake's dependents. Three hundred species of birds including eagles, roadrunners, owls, valley quail and hundreds of songbirds shared space with the numerous waterfowl ranging from ducks and geese to shore birds.

Every small creature from cottontail and squirrel to porcupine and skunk scattered and fed on the flat grassy floor which too had its transition. Away from the river and lake, the prairie supported perennial bunchgrasses, an assortment of needlegrasses, bluegrass and fescue. The damp winters brought peppergrass and plantain which remained green for that period, while the blistering summer grew parched-brown tarweeds. During the short-lived spring months, the prairie took on the look of an artist's colorful palette. Flowering perennials which sprung up in the prairie included mariposa lily, wild onion, buttercups, goldfields, owl's clover, and beardtongue, and were dominated by the vibrant orange of the California poppy. Just as the water levels of the lake changed with the seasons, so did the wildlife living around the lake and river. Antelope, mule deer, and tule elk covered the floor, grazing upon the grassy plains as they migrated from the snowy mountains. Grizzly and black bears, too, ventured as far as the lake to raise their young.

All of these varieties of life shaped a generous landscape which brought a unique richness to the region. Because of this opulence its indigenous people, the Yokuts and Miwoks, became among the largest regional population density in pre-European North America. As an early unknown trapper in the region observed in 1832,

> The population of the extensive valley was so great that it caused surprise, and required a close investigation into the nature of the country that without cultivation, could afford the means of subsistence to so great a community, and who were such indifferent hunters. The causes were found to be multifarous. The abundance and variety of game, of fowl and fish; of the first, elk, bear, deer, antelope, hare and rabbits; of the second, were myriads of geese, embracing four varieties, and from the living rivers of fish,

through all the diminishing varieties from the speckled salmon to the pale perch, were drawn the supplies of life. And yet, the demand for food would have been but partially satisfied had they not brought the vegetable kingdom under contribution. The great variety of number, owing to the climate, of bulbous roots, the seeds of all the grasses, even the tender plants; the fruits of all the perennials, from the lofty pine of the mountains and the oak of the valleys, down through the smaller shrubs that of themselves bear seed for food, being still insufficient for their wants, the noxious buckeye and the kernals of pulpous fruits were brought under requisition, and by the simple process of leaching rendered inoccious [sic] and made palatable and nutritious.

The Indians' lives reflected their harmony with the natural landscape. Seasons, celebrations, and dwellings were determined by their surroundings. A respect for the land existed with these people that is questionable with the inhabitants who followed. Plants were cared for as grasses were seeded and domestic trees were pruned and transplanted. Indians practiced controlled burns which increased the production and the quality of these food sources without harming their most valuable nutrient, the acorn of the valley oak.

Although written accounts of the valley's landscape did not exist until Europeans crossed its floor, historians speculate that what the first white people saw was near to the way the Indians viewed it upon their arrival eons before. This swiftly changed. The prolific landscape, it proved time and again, sustained the abuses and bleeding that the white man continually imposed. The Indian population was the first alteration to the landscape at the hands of the white man. At the time the Spanish first settled in California, it is speculated there were over 20,000 Native Americans living in the Tulare Lake region. This decreased to 500 less than 200 years later. A fellow hunter, in the same party as the trapper who wrote of his wonder at the great numbers of Indians in the region, wrote the following account just one year later:

> On our return, late in the summer of 1833, we found the valleys depopulated. From the head of the Sacramento, to the great bend and slough of the San Joaquin, we did not see more than six or eight live Indians; while large numbers of their skulls and dead bodies were to be seen under almost every shade tree, near water, where the uninhabited and deserted villages had been converted into graveyards . . .

The Miwok tribe, the first to come in contact with the white men, had all but vanished, while the Yokuts somehow barely survived. The one village the trappers found still holding its numbers was located on the Kings River.

THE FIRST WHITE men to actually see the valley were renegades, Spanish soldiers who began deserting their posts along the coast and headed inland. They fled to the open wilderness, which, in its vastness, sheltered the men from discovery. The reason for their desertion is unknown, but what this act did was begin a long chain of events which led one group after another into California's San Joaquin

Valley, each looking for something different, something the land would provide again and again.

Pedro Fages, known as an energetic and rugged hunter and future governor of Spanish California, was the Spanish commander in charge of the expedition intended to bring the soldiers back to their settlements for sentencing. Fages' accounts of his journey through the valley gave the world its first portrait of this land unknown to the white population. He described the valley as,

> a labyrinth of lakes and tulares . . . In the midst of the winding of the River and on the sides there are large rises of land of good soil where with easy irrigation ditches could be made . . . There is also plentiful game, such as deer, antelope, mule deer, bears, geese, cranes ducks and many other species of animal, both terrestrial and winged.

This sketch, written in 1772, roused the Spanish missionaries who had already been spreading Christianity to the Indian people up and down the coastline. The first of an eventual 21 missions was built in San Diego just three years prior, in 1769. This was quickly followed by Mission San Carlos in 1770, Missions San Antonio and San Gabriel in 1771 and Mission San Luis Obispo founded the same year as Fages' narrative. A large population of people in the valley, along with what seemed ample food and supplies, was promising. Soon missionary expeditions were sent out looking for the best mission site. Further explorations were the result of the search for yet more deserters, this time Indian neophytes fleeing their coastal missionary homes. Ironically, the wilderness of the valley's open plains was once again a good hiding place.

In the end, the time and energy spent by the missionaries was to no avail. The clashes which ensued in trying to capture the escaped Indians, who the Spanish considered small and effeminate men, were deadly to the missionaries and their soldiers. Once the neophytes were found, confrontations turned into battles which ended in much blood lost on both sides and without any significant captures. Their encounter with the valley's landscape also proved unworkable. Mission sites in areas that would physically be possible, where there was considerable water, lumber, and food supplies, were not acceptable because of the threat of hostile Indians. Presidios, which would also have to be built, were too costly. Other sites, possibly among amicable Indians, lacked sufficient water or wood, while willows along the many riverbanks lacked durability and size. Thirty-four years after Fages, future head of the San Miguel Mission, Father Cabot, wrote of his 1806 expedition to survey the Kings River:

> The Kings River carries a great deal of water and of a quality which has no equal. There are good lands and a lot of it fit for cultivation, but in all these lands that I went over there is no timber except a few willows along the banks of the river; neither is there any rock; and they say there is none within twenty leagues distant, which is probably true. From what I saw and from what they say, there are a great many Indians, and I think there would be none who would not wish to be baptized. May God produce a means that it may be attained—Amen.

The most favorable spot found for a mission was near present Mooney Grove which had a considerable supply of lumber, but this spot, it was soon learned, also had its drawbacks. The grove was full of California white oak, which are large, striking trees but worthless wood when it came to building, a fact which has spared the oaks which still stand in isolated groves and along the river banks today.

The inability to build a mission in the San Joaquin Valley was not for want of trying. The final strike against the hopeful missionaries came in the 1820s as a wave of Spanish revolutionary wars began. This deprived Spain of most of its colonies and fortune. Other than the baptizing of many Indians in the process, these expeditions were futile. Spain's opportunity for progress in the valley was lost forever. The last California mission, Mission San Francisco, was built in 1823.

It is difficult to speculate how a successful mission site in this region would have had any bearing on the eventual alteration of the landscape. There is no question that with the coming of a white population the wild land was destined to be tamed into arable farmland. One can only guess whether this change would have occurred any sooner or with any degree of discretion. The one thing for certain is the consequence of these first accounts of the region's landscape.

The value of the written word has been the one constant in the allure and change of the valley floor. What these viewers did not know was that as they wrote they were recording for the last time the landscape they saw. After that the land was altered by the next visionary who read these writings and headed west. The descriptions of the valley and its resources documented by Pedro Fages and Father Cabot led trappers and hunters to become the valley's next inhabitants.

3

And stepping westward seemed to be
A kind of heavenly destiny
                    —William Wordsworth,
                              Stepping Westward

AT THE TIME Spanish missionaries were first traversing the San Joaquin Valley's floor, some of my ancestors were already settled in the American colonies. These were the Beaver and, my namesake, the Apperson lines of my family. Accordingly, it would be descendants of these two families that would eventually make their way to the San Joaquin Valley and become some of the region's earliest white settlers.

The Beaver line was notorious for constant moving, perhaps always looking forward, and in most cases westward, for a better life, more space, and freedom. For some generations they had a reason to move, and for others they seemed to create one.

In the early 18th century, Johannes de Beauvoir, a Huguenot, left Luray, France, after King Louis XIV's 1685 revocation of the Edict of Nantes which once again placed

French Protestants in peril. The de Beauvoirs and other Protestant families fled to Deux Ponts, Alsace, then German territory. There the family name changed to Bieber. Once the family finally settled in Berks County, Pennsylvania in 1740, the name became Beaver. Even here, in new and free territory of Pennsylvania, their stay was but a short one. It took only three more generations before Johannes' great-grandson, Henry Beaver, would leave his home in Missouri and step foot on California soil.

Although I do not know all the arrival dates of my family's other 126 lines of this era, it is doubtful that any of them were here before the Appersons. This family left Wales for the colonies in 1648. Unlike the Beavers, the Appersons' reason for departure is unclear. They may have fled from Oliver Cromwell if they were loyal to King Charles I or similarly escaped because of religious persecution. But my intuition tells me that, if they were anything like their American descendants, they came to the colonies for the adventure and for the free land given to settlers. It is known they had land in southern Wales and had at least some money since their children attended public school. Nothing suggests that they were driven from their home. Perhaps the only thing driven was what turned inside them as they set out for a new land. Crossing the Atlantic meant a prosperous new beginning and was possibly a romantic idea as well.

Adverse to my antecedents' expectancy, tragedy struck early in the voyage when both parents died and were buried at sea. Left behind were four orphaned boys facing a homeless arrival in the new land of Yorke County, later to be known as New Kent County, Virginia. The youngest, William, was described in the parish records as a "poor lad

[with] a sore leg" and was the first of the boys to be taken in by others. William is my sixth-great-grandfather.

With each generation these families moved, at first one county at a time west from Berks and New Kent Counties. After the years of the Revolutionary War the distances became greater as Beavers and Appersons were being born in Ohio, Indiana, Illinois, and Missouri. Other branches such as the Pecks left Virginia for Tennessee, the Owens for Kentucky, and the Gasaways for Indiana. Still more branches arrived in Kansas and Oklahoma to secure homestead land.

Along the way they lived off the land and grew customarily large families, a few prosperous but mostly poor, some even leaving marks among the annals of American history. Abraham Owen died in the Battle of Tippecanoe while his son, Clark Lewis, died in the bloodiest of Civil War battles, Shiloh. Colonel Upton Hays was leader of Missouri's Twelfth Confederate Calvary, many of his men riding with Quantrill during those bloodiest of raids on Union settlements. Although known as the fastest gun in the west, according to Ripley's, and hero of the Battle of Lone Jack, he was shot through the head just one year after this triumph. His family, for he was Daniel Boone's great-grandson and my great-great-grandfather, was from Missouri. Hays' family, including his daughter, my great-grandmother Elfleda Hays Apperson, came to California from Missouri on the first transcontinental train.

The most documented of these families is Elfleda's. Not only was this historical train voyage recorded by her cousin who came West with her family, but Elfleda's mother, Margaret Watts Hays' correspondence with her husband and parents has also been preserved. Over 100 letters chronicling the Civil War, its tense prelude and toilsome aftermath, remain. She writes anguishing letters to her parents and brothers living in the Sierra Nevada mining town of Mariposa in the 1850s and 1860s. Desperate to be rejoined with her parents and brothers, her letters include accounts of Jayhawkers, Union renegades, burning down four of her Missouri homes, while letters from her husband, Upton, describe the life he wishes for them west of Missouri and the war. A widow with four children, it wasn't until 1872 that she finally had the means to arrive in California, money from her family's meager mine allowing her the passage. This trip, which took only five days, fulfilled Margaret's dream of settling in California, a dream she had had for nearly 25 years.

The greatest enticement for movement west came with the discovery of gold in California's hills. It is what led men from Margaret Watts Hays' family as well as those from the Beaver and Apperson lines to California, and, more successfully, this is what brought George Hearst and his young bride, Phoebe Apperson Hearst, to California where they amassed a fortune in mining. Phoebe, born in Missouri, was my great-grandfather's cousin. Contrary to his cousin-in-law, my great-grandfather's attempt at mining left him nearly penniless. It was money from the Hearst Corporation that paid for his funeral, saving him from a pauper's grave.

Although the outcomes and struggles of these people differed, one constant remained. Being among the earliest settlers in uncharted land has been a reoccurrence in my family's history.

In the same year Pedro Fages was writing down his first sketches of the Kings River and Tulare Lake landscape, Daniel Boone, my fifth-great-grandfather, was trudging his way through the Appalachian wilderness into the Ohio Valley, presently Kentucky. These steps led the way for the westward movement. Boone has been nicknamed The Pathfinder, but what he did was so much more. He not only set trails but a precedent that a nation would follow. Boone became the romanticized leader of the values the young country placed on wilderness which was to explore and claim. Land was, and continues to be, the most prized of possessions. Because of the actions of Boone and others like him, nature was tamed acre by acre as an agrarian landscape replaced the native fields and settlers fed on the earth's abundance.

As each generation was born, they grew just as restless as the last and moved farther west, always west. In studying a genealogical pedigree chart the size of my coffee table, I follow their names filtering down to my solitary name on the far left of the chart. If I place a translucent map of the United States over it, I can read the parallels between the two as I look right to left, east to west, as I trace their movement toward the Pacific.

The question I keep asking is why my family, all of them, continued moving west. Others, who arrived in the same years, stayed in the comfort of the eastern states. Had they found a sense of home, a reassurance of place, which was missing in my own bloodline? For five generations now my family has lived in one state. This is longer than any has settled before. But then, this was the end of the American wilderness.

4

December 22nd. This is the Lake Fork; one of the largest and handsomest streams in the valley, being about one hundred yards broad and having perhaps a larger body of fertile lands than any one of the others. It is called by the Mexicans the Rio de los Reyes. The broad alluvial bottoms were well wooded with several species of oaks. This is the principal affluent of the Tulare Lake, a strip of water which receives all the rivers in the upper or southern end of the valley. In time of high water it discharges into the San Joaquin River, making a continuous water-line through the whole extent of the valley. The lake itself is surrounded by lowlands and its immediate shores are rankly overgrown with bulrushes.

—John C. Fremont,
Memoirs of My Life

LEGENDARY JEDIDIAH SMITH made the first white man's overland visit to the valley via an eastern route through the Great Basin and Mojave Desert. Born in New

York, his family, reminiscent of my own, moved continually west in the desire to stay on the edge of wilderness. As a child, Smith read the journals of Lewis and Clark and is quoted as saying, "I wanted to be the first to view a country on which the eye of a white man had never gazed and to follow the course of rivers that run through a new land." This region met his desire. He trapped beavers and otters in the Tulare and Kern Lakes. In 1826, while there, he named the former lake the Two Larres and wrote in his journal, "'I found a few beaver, and elk, deer, and antelope in abundance,'" confirming the missionaries' accounts. The Canadian-established Hudson Bay Company paid Smith $20,000 for the furs he trapped that season. The obvious quality and quantity of goods in the valley soon brought more white men into the region. After Smith other trappers traversed the valley floor, including famed trappers Joseph Walker (part of the 1833 Bonneville expedition which crossed into California through the Sierra) and Ewing Young (who came through the Mojave Desert near the same time), and at least sixty men from the Hudson Bay Company and many French trappers. These men never considered creating a permanent post in the vicinity for fur trading. They instead pillaged and left. In fact, Ewing Young reported upon traveling up and down the San Joaquin Valley that it was already "trapped out."

By the mid 1800s, the beaver were almost all depleted. Gone too were other pelt-bearing animals, the mink and otter. Bears no longer migrated to the lake, leaving the famed bear hunter, Grizzly Adams (also a native of New York) to hunt tule elk and water fowl.

Adams documented the following on a hunt at Pelican Island, located where the Kings River met Tulare Lake. The year was 1854:

On the (west) borders of the lake, near the
mouth of the Kings River, there was an Indian
village . . . and I engaged two boys of them to
take me to an island in the lake, where there
was said to be elk in abundance, and birds of
various kinds in astonishing plenty . . . . we
crossed an arm of the lake, and landed on a
small wooded island, which was a place of birds
indeed. There were birds in almost incredible
numbers—ducks, geese, swans, cranes, curlews,
snipes, and various other kinds, in all stages of
growth, and eggs by thousands among the grass
and tules . . . . and we saw also elk in numbers
which fled into the tules at our approach . . . .
Soon afterwards we embarked again in the
canoe, with the fawn, the slaughtered elks, and
an immense quantity of young birds and eggs,
and returned to the village, where the Indians
gathered around, discussed our successful
hunting with great interest. Altogether, this
island hunt was as pleasant and interesting to
me as any I had enjoyed during the season.

The depletion of wild game was the beginning of the
next turn in what was to become of the remaining wilderness.
The Indians and Indian neophytes who also suffered due to
the overhunting from white trappers delivered the answer
to this change: cattle. The neophytes had been trained as
vaqueros and in 1837 made their first of many cattle raids
on already existing coastal ranches. The "Two Larres," later
to be known as Tulare Lake, became the terminal for cattle
before driving them east. The watery tule lands around

this area were broken up by large expanses of naturally grassy meadows that were a salvation for cattle before their departure.

The change in vegetation caused by the introduction of European grasses by the Spanish fifty years before created an opportune landscape for cattle. This, along with the depletion of wild game and the scarcity of available grazing land on the coast due to expanding cattle stock, made men eager to accept land grants in the San Joaquin Valley frontier. Soon many trappers, seeing their earnings decreasing along with the animals, became cattlemen, bringing to the valley its next change of scenery. Prior to US statehood, the system for acquiring land was a simple appeal to the Mexican governor that included a hand-drawn map of the boundaries and natural features. Expansive areas of land were routinely granted, sometimes resulting in the ownership of land covering thousands of acres. Soon, the open ranges were filled with tens of thousands of roaming cattle, the legendary Miller and Lux cattle operation monopolizing this market.

Yet another New Yorker, William Brewer, a geologist and chemist by trade, joined the first California Geological Survey in 1860 just months after his wife's and infant son's deaths. His mission was to take botanical surveys on mostly unexplored regions, the Kings River and Tulare Lake regions among them. Brewer was meticulous in his work of testing soil and mapping terrain, leaving behind several manuscripts and notebooks. One account dated June 2 states, "We came upon green plains, green with fine rushes, called wire grass, and some alkali grass. The ground is wetter and cattle can live on the rushes and grass." These accounts of native grasses led men to bring more cattle to the region.

In these early days of ranching, the natural landscape remained much as it was before. The prairie grasslands were abundant in feed; therefore, no crops were needed for their keep. These usually large tracts of land that were so easily acquired needed no fencing to block the cattle or the landscape's flow. Water was abundant and oak trees which dotted the plains provided shelter for the animals. The following account is a record of a trip made by Captain John Barker in August of 1856 as he decided to develop a livestock ranch along the Kings River:

> We went equipped with a wagon, almost like a house on wheels, with a large cover. Each man had also a saddle horse, and the wagon was driven by four gentle oxen that were accustomed to camp life and would stay wherever camp was made without much herding. With the horses it was different; they had to be brought into camp every night, hobbled, and tied up short and grass gathered for their feeds in order to keep the bands of wild horses, of which there were thousands on the Fresno plains, from stampeding them and running off with the wild bands, and, if they once get away with them, they were apparently wilder than the wildest and fully as difficult to recapture . . . .

> The plain all along the margin of the swamp for forty miles was covered with a heavy growth of grass that waved in the wind like a field of grain. The ground was thickly strewed with the horns of the elk where they annually shed them and a good many entire skulls with head

or horns of bull elk that had been killed by hunters. Those were all bleached white as snow. I took my horse and riata and dragged up an immense pile and piled them up about eight feet high so that they could be readily seen a mile or more away. I established this mark so that the place could be easily and readily found again as there were no natural marks there, and I then and there determined that I would locate there and would develop one of the best stock ranches in the valley.

The Spanish longhorns were the first cattle brought by the Spanish missionaries. This was when the need for hide was more important than the need for beef. As the population in the region grew, the need for better beef cattle also increased. The new cattlemen began to import Hereford and Shorthorn cattle along with the Holstein dairy cow. Still, the natural environment was a challenge to the new ranchers. One animal which remained in abundance in the valley was the coyote, an animal with a unique way of taking its prey. When a coyote encircled these new and prosperous beef cattle, they would likewise keep turning to face the coyote, eventually becoming dizzy and falling to the ground at which time their calves would be free for the coyote to kill. The same fate would not occur with the long-horn, which would merely turn its head from side to side until the coyote moved on to easier prey. This usually occurred near the river where food for the coyote was readily available.

As with the cows and coyotes, the ranchers too usually occupied the land nearest the river bottoms due to the naturally green vegetation. William Brewer describes in his journal the more hospitable location:

> About six miles from Kings River we struck a
> belt of scattered oaks—fine trees—and what a
> relief! For, except a few cragged willows, shrubs
> rather than trees, in places along the sloughs,
> we had seen no trees for the last 130 miles of
> the trip!

It was published information such as this that began leading larger amounts of settlers moving west, searching for expanses of unobstructed, arable land.

As early as 1844, expeditions into California were no longer in search of fur but to gather more extensive topographical and geographical information. Another observer of the area's flora and fauna was John Woodhouse Audubon, son of famed wildlife artist John James Audubon. His mission was to continue his father's work, a man who wrote passionately about bird habitats. In his *Western Journal* of 1849 and 1850 John Woodhouse Audubon noted:

> [*No date.*] *Tulare Valley.* One more day brought
> us to this great valley, and the view from the
> last hill looking to northwest was quite grand,
> stretching on one hand until lost in distance,
> and on the other the snowy mountains on the
> east of the Tulare valley. Here, for the first time,
> I saw the Lewis woodpecker, and Steller's jay
> in this country. I have seen many California
> vultures and a new hawk, with a white tail and
> red shoulders. During the dry season this great
> plain may be travelled on, but now numerous

> ponds and lakes exist, and the ground is in
> places, for miles, too boggy to ride over, so we
> were forced to skirt the hills.

Gathering substantial information about the region was of interest to the east, the nation's capital in particular. The territory was proving itself an increasingly valuable landscape due to its open cattle range, mostly benign Native American population, and most importantly, discovery of gold. If Mexico were to lose control of California, the United States government wanted to secure it before England, France, or Russia had the chance.

John Fremont was the man chosen for the job. Prior to Fremont's stints as Abraham Lincoln's appointed Civil War major general, Military Governor and California Senator, he was a California land-owner. He bought his 44,000 acre parcel, Las Mariposa, from the last California-Mexican Governor in 1844.

Fremont hired Kit Carson as a guide. Carson was, along with Fremont, a popular hero of his time. This was in part due to public reports of their gainful expeditions, accounts of the San Joaquin Valley among them. Fremont and Carson headed west along with an additional band of frontiersmen. Upon entering the San Joaquin Valley, Fremont was immediately enamored. It was April, when the lupine and poppies were in full bloom and the grasses were their short-lived green. A few months earlier, he would have become lost in the tule fog that at times hangs to the ground all day. A few months later and he would have gasped at the valley's heat. What he saw was the valley in its prime, prime of season and prime of era. He wrote in his journal of April fifth, sixth, and seventh:

During the earlier part of the day's ride, the country presented a lacustrine appearance; the river was deep, and nearly on a level with the surrounding country; its banks raised like a levee, and fringed with willows. Over the bordering plain were interspersed spots of prairie among fields of *tule* (bullrushes,) which in this country are called *tulares* and little ponds . . . . Riding on through the timber, about dark we found abundant water in small ponds, 20 to 30 yards in diameter, with clear deep water and sandy beds, bordered with bogrushes, (*juncus effusus*,) and a tall rush (*scirpus lacustris*) 12 feet high, and surrounded near the margin with willow trees in bloom; among them one which resembled *salix myricoides*. The oak of the groves was the same already mentioned, with small leaves, in form like those of the white oak, and forming, with the evergreen oak, the characteristic trees of the valley.

Fremont gave to occupants of the civilized east, possibly some of my ancestors among them, accurate and vivid descriptions of the land out west. His narrative style no doubt induced many with similar adventurist dreams to go west to see the lupines and poppies for themselves. "One might travel the whole world over," Fremont wrote, "without finding a valley more fresh and verdant—more floral and sylvan—more alive with birds and animals—more bounteously watered—than we had left in the San Joaquin."

Six years after Fremont's first account of the valley, California had become a state, and Fremont was one of the valley's early cattle kings, although it took another six years for the American government to accept his Mexican Land Grant. The land that he had so beautifully described as floral and sylvan had changed in a matter of a few years by the overabundance of hunters, trappers and eventually cattlemen such as he.

THESE CHANGES NOT only impacted the natural landscape but the native people who had lived upon it for so long. Since so little is left here in the valley pertaining to the American Indians' way of life, it is very easy to forget, or never even learn, that this culture existed. When we hear about the hostilities between the white man and Native Americans, the events take place on the plains and deserts leading to California, but not often in California. With the emergence of cattle ranching in the valley, hostilities with the Indians ensued. The valley witnessed massacres, raids, ambushes, and reprisals "as merciless as any of those recorded in Kentucky annals." Fremont was at times in the middle of such episodes. While many ranchers were killed, many more Native Americans were left dead. The tide of reorder upon the land was surging.

After the US won the war with Mexico, the 1851 Governor, Peter Burnett, urged that the Native population was to be relocated east of the Sierra. If they were not, "a war of extermination will continue to be waged until the Indian race should become extinct." Several treaties were signed with the Yokuts promising them reservation land in the southern valley. However, in 1852, the US Senate rejected these treaties. The short-lived reservation land was now available to settlers. This only ensued more hostility between settlers and the Yokuts, resulting in skirmishes near Visalia and at Fort Tejon, with the most notable being the Tule River War at Battle Mountain. The first half of the 19th century brought pneumonia, diphtheria, measles, and malaria epidemics. During the second half of that century and into the 20th, countless numbers were killed and removed from their homes along the Kings River and Tulare Lake regions.

The editor of the Los Angeles *Star* stated the following response to the short-lived treaties:

> To place upon our most fertile soil the degrade race of aboriginals upon the North American continent, to invest them with the rights of sovereignty, and to teach them that they are to be treated as powerful and independent nations, is planting the seeds of future disaster and ruin.

In looking at the destruction of flora and fauna of this region that came as a result of the white man's migration, it is unimaginable to believe that these "seeds of disaster and ruin" could have ever been speculated as being at the hands of the Yokuts.

5

It will be but a short time until this section will be in a high state of cultivation and present an appearance of prosperity unequaled in the State. No such thing as failure of crops is ever known, as King's River always carries a vast amount of water. The rapid advancement made by the settlers in this portion of the county, together with their many public enterprises, demonstrates the fact that the desert can be made to blossom as the rose.

— *History of Tulare County, California*

THE DISAPPEARANCE OF wild game on the valley floor, in effect, allowed livestock into the region. However, the event which made cattle ranching prosper beyond expectations did not occur in the valley but miles away in the Sierra Nevada. This was the discovery of gold. The alteration of the valley's landscape began in the hills above it, when as if overnight thousands came to the newly secured territory in search of gilded veins and nuggets which they could take back east with them. John Watts, my great-great-grandmother's brother, described the following to her in a letter written June 20th, 1850 from his Sierra Nevada mining camp:

> You want to hear something about California. I will tell you what I think of it. California Certainly is the best Country in the world, it lacks nothing but good society. The vallys are the most beautifull Scenery in the world . . . . and the greatest variety of Beautiful flowers that Ever you Saw in your life covers the hole of the land. Sickness is allmost unknown in this Country to the old Settlers . . . . It is the most healthy country that ever I saw.

It has been estimated that within the five year gold rush period 300,000 men and women ventured to California. The Watts family, which included my great-great-great grandparents, John and Elizabeth Berry Watts, secured land in Mariposa, a part of John Fremont's Spanish Land Grant. The branding iron which John Watts used for his cattle was acquired from Fremont. Although the family would hold onto this land into the next century, the large extended family that arrived seeking gold found a more prosperous life in the valley, and so many of them settled in the towns of the Tulare Lake Basin, Hanford, Lemoore, and Armona, among them.

The necessary supply of food for the miners became a boom for ranchers in this region and soon hogs and sheep too became commonplace on the valley floor. "No stock in this country is more easily reared, or multiplies so rapidly as swine," writes Titus Cronise in his 1868 book titled *The Natural Wealth of California*, a collection of propaganda of sorts intended to lure people from their eastern homes. This painted the valley as a place of abundance and opportunity. One section states: "In many places where the soil is thin, oak and other trees supply vast ranges of mass feed." For those growing weary of panning or who had to provide more substantial means for a family, these descriptions were promising. Other, more successful, prospects were available.

Hog drives coincided with cattle drives to the mines hundreds of miles away. Most of these hogs were razorbacks or "tule splitters" as they were known in the San Joaquin Valley. With such large numbers of hogs roaming the unfenced valley, many became unaccounted for as they settled along the abundant rivers feeding on tules, grass and roots. Around the shores of Tulare Lake hogs fed on clams which were, in places, several feet thick. It was reported the hogs even dove for them. Though the indigenous animals were by this point thinned out, this introduced domestic animal became new "wild" game.

As with any overabundance in the natural landscape, the outcome is not only detrimental but lasting. Added to this, with the numbers of cattle growing every day, the once available space, water, and natural protection for these animals became limited. The once abundant bunch grasses suffered from the feeding and trampling of the stock. This was when many ranchers began to look to sheep as an answer, just as harmful ecologically, but more economically sound. Sheep could exist in the dry hot elements that often devastated cattle. Cronise claimed, "California is, perhaps, the best country in the world, excepting Australia, for the raising of sheep. Nowhere do they thrive and multiply with so little care; and no fleeces of similar breeds are so heavy." These prospects were almost too good to be true. By the turn of the century, the town of my grandmother's youth,

Lemoore, became the nation's number one wool shipping point. This growth may have been one more factor for my great-grandparents Beaver's move from their own sheep ranch in Santa Rosa 200 miles to the north and their planting of alfalfa in their new home.

While a few men made their riches in the mining towns, many became penniless and filtered their way down into the valley below which promised some kind of living. Although ranchers and miners continued their disdain for each other, the fact remained that they depended on one another for their prosperity. By the early 1850s, regular wagon roads traversed the valley floor in all directions.

Three prosperous but short years after the discovery of gold, prices for sheep and cattle began to fall as the large numbers of livestock being herded into the state flooded the market. This, coupled with the lessening demand for beef from the increasingly fatigued miners, brought a fall to the trade. With this decline, as with the abatement of wild game, the landscape would have to be altered once again if it was to continue thriving. Up to this point, the cattle rancher held a hierarchical position in the region. According to the "No Fence" or "Trespass" law a rancher's cattle could invade a farmer's orchard and destroy it, leaving the farmer no legal recourse. This all changed in the year 1874, conveniently the same year barbed wire was invented. The open range was closed when it was decided that ranchers would be held accountable for damage their stock had inflicted on a neighboring farmer's field. At this time, there were nearly three hundred thousand head of cattle and one million sheep in the valley. The money required to fence these numbers on ranches that covered such enormous areas was not feasible, even to the wealthy ranchers. This decision was another blow to the already suffering ranchers.

What was equally damaging were the consequences of having so many head of cattle, hogs, and sheep in the region. The overgrazing that ensued was disastrous. William Brewer continues his account of cattle ranching in the region observing, "We now came on thousands of them that have retreated to this feed and have gnawed it almost to the earth." Sheep and hogs ate below the plain's grasses and into the roots, leaving the soil unprotected and completely barren.

As with the trappers and hunters who overhunted the valley just fifty years before, the ranchers too had used the valley to the point of destruction. Natural vegetation had been overrun with introduced European grasses on which their livestock fed. Native bunchgrasses could not compete with these new grasses that were brought in rather accidentally by the Spanish explorers years before. What was once one of the more diverse grasslands in North America was compromised. If the settlers wanted to continue to live in the valley, their energies had to be turned toward something else. This would be farming.

THE ERA OF exploration was over and with it the natural state these pioneers found. The changes to the landscape in the form of crops and irrigation canals would last into the present day; its progress so pervasive that the natural landscape is today unrecognizable. The expanse and possibilities of the valley clouded the viewer's eye with expectations which did not last. William Brewer prophetically recorded the following on an April day near Visalia:

> But this plain is the great feature. The mountains are so dim in the east that they are not conspicuous, so that the plain seems as

interminable as the ocean, except on the west. The ground is already dry, the grass very scanty and seldom over two or three inches high. As it grew hotter a mirage flitted around us—a great lake of clear water continually before us for hours. Once the appearance was so deceptive that we took the wrong road, supposing that it led around the water we thought was ahead of us. It took us out of the way, so that we did not strike the right road for some miles. You can have no idea of the extraordinary optical and atmospheric phenomenon. The eye is so deceived that the understanding refuses to dissent from the apparent truth.

The valley was a mirage of sorts in which a different image appeared in the shimmering horizon for each person. Mirage has become a reliable metaphor when looking at the history of this valley and those who wished to prosper here. The apparent truth is that the land could not withstand what these trappers, missionaries, and ranchers wished the land to continue to be for them. As the illusion receded what remained was an altered landscape.

6

*The whole gigantic sweep of the San Joaquin
expanded, Titanic, before the eye of the mind,
flagellated in heat, quivering and shimmering
under the sun's red eye. At long intervals, a faint
breath of wind out of the south passed slowly
over the levels of the baked and empty earth,
accentuating the silence, marking off the stillness.
It seemed to exhale from the land itself, a prolonged
sigh as of deep fatigue.*

—Frank Norris,
The Octopus

THE DIVISION OF land into private hands began in
California as early as 1784 when Mexican Governor Pedro
Fages introduced the land-grant system. This institution,
however, was not practiced in the San Joaquin Valley until
the year 1843. With the emergence of ranching in the region,
boundaries had to be set. This first wave of sectioning off
land in the valley took on large masses of ground (thousands
to tens of thousands of acres) that eventually were scaled
down time and time again until the present day.

Acquiring a portion of land was extremely easy for the Mexican descendants who laid the first claim to the land. The first land grant of this area, owned by Manuel Castro, was called the Laguna de Tache and was located just south of the Kings River in present-day Kings and Tulare counties. It consisted of 48,800.62 acres and was easily obtained using scarce guidelines. Only a few regulations for land grants were demanded: no individual grant could be over eleven square leagues, and these leagues be divided into one league of irrigable soil, four dependent upon rainfall, and six acceptable for grazing. No maps of prospective land grants were required. Boundaries were decided by using fixed markers, which in the valley were few and far between. It was miles between oaks, rivers and sloughs, or the foothills of the surrounding Sierra Nevada and Coast Range mountains. Hence, the enormous size of some of the land grants. In the case of Laguna de Tache, it was bound on the north by the Kings River, the south by Cross Creek and lay in between the Sierra and Tulare Lake. Other land grant boundaries were often less vague, such as one whose southern limit was "by the place where Don Simeon Castro sits on his horse each evening," or other unreliable markers, such as oak trees which had been chopped down. With land this plentiful, accurate surveys were not important. The following is a description of the surveying method:

> One man placed his stake in the ground and the other set out at a gallop to the end of the rope. Then the first man pulled up his stake and rode past his partner to the end of the rope. They continued riding and stopping in this manner until they had enclosed enough land

> to approximate the number of square leagues
> contained in the grant. In case the grass was wet
> the rawhide lariat would stretch considerably
> and the grantee would receive rather generous
> boundaries.

When war broke out with Mexico, these Californios held fast to their lands, refusing to take their homeland's side. The Guadalupe-Hidalgo treaty was signed in 1848, ending the war and giving California and most of the southwest territory to US control. The treaty contained two important articles deciding the fate of Mexican ranchers in the valley. In effect, they could remain in residence, their ranches intact. The other article made them United States citizens if they were determined to stay on their land. Researchers have estimated that in the 12 years between 1834 and 1846, the Mexican government granted more than seven hundred private grants in the whole of California. Thus, most of the desirable land, including that in the valley, was in the hands of private owners.

Near this same time, the San Joaquin Valley was merely a stopping point for many first settlers coming across land routes from the east. Those who did not have their hopes set on gold were headed toward the newly prosperous coastal communities, from San Francisco to Los Angeles, which were teeming with cattle ranches. Despite the wide-open land of the valley, these people took what they could use and moved through without consideration of staying. After completing the treacherous trip across the Sierra, which often threatened their lives, the settlers made camp in the flat lands below to rest and regroup. The hunger that they experienced during their descent into the valley subsided as they feasted on what remained of the valley's wild game.

Fed and rested, they moved on, across the broad expanse of the valley and into the Coast Range Mountains to their new homes in what they considered to be the promised California.

In just a few years' time, however, overgrazing on the coast, along with the repeal of the "no fence" law which had been a deterrent to the settlers, made these newcomers reassess the land in the valley. The land was wide open, well-populated with grasses, and, in some regions, free.

In 1850 Congress had passed the Swamp Land Act which enabled the state to acquire two million acres of overflow land near the often-swelling rivers. This land was then turned around and sold to prospective farmers for $1.25 an acre. If the settler would give proof to the government that he had spent another $1.25 an acre on land reclamation, the purchase price would be refunded. This being too tempting a deal to new settlers, some reportedly placed a rowboat upon their buckboard and sat in the boat while touring the acreage. They could then "truthfully" report to the government that they had traversed their land in a boat. When officials later inspected the land to find it dry, they gave back the $1.25.

Once the territory was secured under U.S. control, government surveyors tried their best to make these boundaries accurate by using the rectangular survey system. Beginning in 1851 under the Land Act, these titles to the land had to be validated, a costly and inconvenient endeavor on the part of the land owner. But as area historian, Wallace Smith, states in his elemental history of the San Joaquin Valley, *Garden of the Sun*, "Individual unhappiness was not so much the result of a change in government as it was the pain which is a necessary concomitant to growth and development." Those unable to finance the hearings and presentation of claims before the federal courts went bankrupt or merely gave up their holdings.

The rectangular survey system method "required that claims in the national domain be bounded by lines directed to the cardinal points of the compass." Based on a grid system, the land was subdivided into square townships, square miles, and fractions of square miles. These fractions promoted the advancement of family farms. By the year 1855, most of this region was divided. As was the case during Mexican control, the value of the parcels of land, no matter the straightness and accuracy of their lines, was judged by topographical characteristics. If there was a lack of natural vegetation or water, the land was less valuable than a parcel containing oaks, a stream, and a variety of grasses. The rich soil, the one constant feature of the valley, was not considered. While one surveyor saw green fields in the springtime, an appraiser saw the dried-up stream beds of the hot summer months. Once again in the valley's history, accounts of the landscape would vary with each viewer. The one constant was the quickness with which the land was divided. The sooner this was completed the sooner more settlers could be on the land. Just as the Mexican ranchers had found before, land was easily acquired. The promise of homestead land, coupled with propaganda, persuaded many pioneers to travel west. In his book *Vanishing Landscapes*, William Preston points out,

> An individual could select and claim a parcel of land from a map that showed no sign of the environmental diversity of the basin. An artificial system now structured human relationships to the land, and farmers, rather than attempting to devise a system to accord

with nature, learned to adjust nature to suit the
system.

And adjust nature, they did.

ALTHOUGH THIS UNIFORM division of the land would
have been familiar to many Americans venturing west from
states whose acreage was surveyed likewise, many others
from more distant places might have found this imposition
of angular lines unusual. My great-grandmother's family,
the O'Connors, left the Irish-settled Frampton, Quebec,
in 1852. I have often wondered about the land they left
behind. Were the roads narrow and muddy and did they
curve to follow a river and hills, or meadows and grove of
trees? Was their farm plotted closely the same, with odd
parcels purchased here and there, perhaps by a stream where
their sheep could drink and the division of the land would
round and protrude of its own contour among the rest of
the wilds? Did the moist air keep the soil damp and rich or
did they divert water to feed their farm?

Beginning in 1841, families began leaving Frampton
for California via Missouri. The O'Connors decided on the
ocean course instead of the more linear overland route. The
land passage west was not a direct line, but there was the
attempt. However, there could be no straight lines for a ship
pitching its way around Cape Horn. Ships often spun in
circles for months in the attempt to round the violent cape.
Once in the rolling hills of Santa Rosa, they were confronted
with angularity for possibly the first time. Their home sat
on the southeast corner of the 150 acre square grazing
land. Yet hills surrounded them, seemingly unaffected by
imaginary lines. Twenty years later, homestead land in the
San Joaquin Valley lured them. This brought them one

step further toward the man-made creation of an angular nature. There were no surrounding hills to seemingly break the constancy of square points. Acreage, roads, homes, crop rows fell into the rigidness of east to west and north to south. Their eighty-acre farm existed very near where is now the perpendicular crossing of highways 41 and 198. Eventually railroads too would add to the constant pattern on the valley's floor. And finally the one defined curve of the valley's landscape, the rivers, would also become the straight, devised lines of irrigation canals.

The valley has become as linear as my genealogy chart which tells me where and when my ancestors came to this valley. Lines create order, order which is necessary if every space is not to be lost or wasted. Living among such straight lines, it becomes natural to expect nature to conform to this ungraceful pattern. The slightest curve to a road or bend in a canal catches the eye as being out of place, "unnatural," if you will, in the valley's landscape.

Friends from Great Britain came to visit the valley once and quickly observed that we "have no curves in [our] roads." This was a characteristic which I first observed when I visited their country, where winding lanes were obviously placed before the practice of the rectangular survey. Where they dash into a circular maze of round-a-bouts, we sit in lines of intersections. Where their towns are built beside the sweep of the river, our towns lay according to the confines of a grid.

The Brits found it easy to find their way around the valley. With such compass-driven paths it is difficult to become lost. North is always obvious, something which is not apparent in their country. They were stuck, however, when they tried to drive to the Kings River which was only one mile from our home, and two miles away from the nearest town. Contrary to their home where rivers are accessible by lanes and footpaths, every road they took east was blocked by one running north and south diagonal to the river with crops and private property blocking any access, or view for that matter. Roads constructed along the river's path not only disturb potential cropland but also disrupt the rectangular design of our pavements, a pattern to which we have become so accustomed.

7

There began to settle in this vast valley, in 1848-49, that intrepid band of pioneers who had scaled the Sierra, or sailed 'around the Horn'.
—Titus Fey Cronise,
The Natural Wealth of California

IN MY GRANDMOTHER'S photo album is a sepia photograph mounted on heavy cardboard and rounded on the corners from the many years. It captures my grandmother's two oldest brothers standing on the edge of a newly planted field. On the other side of the camera are the first shoots of alfalfa rising straight atop narrow rows, the patchwork of a newly arable land. Behind the men is the farmhouse, plain and square. The men's overalls harbor dust in turned up cuffs and their hands display deep, dirt-filled lines. The focus of the picture is where their hands rest, on the concrete pump pulling water to their turned field like blood from a vein.

FIFTY YEARS BEFORE this scene, in 1868, Titus Fey Cronise published his *Natural Wealth of California*. It is an extensive almanac of the state's characteristics, from commercial and agricultural possibilities to descriptions of flora and fauna. "The immigrant," writes Cronise, "will meet with some difficulty in seeking a location for a settlement in California of which he should be advised." He warns his audience, mostly being those adventurers from the civilized east, that it is not a landscape for the faint of heart or those desiring an easy profit. For those thinking about living in the San Joaquin Valley, he had this to say:

> The farmer's life in California is unlike that of the Atlantic States. The long summer's drought creates a vast deal of dust, which is sometimes very disagreeable. It covers nearly everything around with a coating that lasts from May to November, and penetrates every crevice. The earth is almost everywhere alkaline, and the air affects the eyes and air passages. Traveling is rendered very unpleasant. Flies and mosquitoes prevail. In the rain season the mud is equally uncomfortable, and wagonering is nearly impracticable. Farms are generally much larger here than at the East and neighbors are far apart. Good water is rare and most of it is alkaline. The absence of barns and the small dwelling houses strike the stranger's eye. But, more than all, there is an apparent want of comfort, which is, however, incident in a measure to all new settlements. This is greatly heightened by the absence of shade trees . . . .

It is a wonder so many arrived.

Once again, accounts of the San Joaquin Valley's landscape varied depending on season and intentions for its use. Where the Spaniards had searched for mission sites, the American easterner looked to cultivate the land into what they considered a civilized inhabitance. Because of the valley's many months of little or no rainfall, many reports by white visitors about the valley still remained unfavorable. One such account was by Lieutenant George H. Derby, a topographical engineer for the United States Army looking for possible military outposts. He described the setting as a "horrible desert" with soil "generally dry, decomposed and incapable of cultivation." He concluded that the valley was

> barren, decomposed, no trace of vegetation but a few straggling artemisias . . . scorpions, centipedes and a small but extremely poisonous rattlesnake about eighteen inches long . . . which, with the gophers and ground rats are the only denizens of this unpleasant and uninhabitable spot.

Twenty-five years after Lieutenant Derby wrote his account the first small acreage farmers, my ancestors included, were breaking their land. As they first dug their ditches and diverted water from the rivers, it was quickly determined that Derby and his contemporaries were wrong. The land, once irrigated, was indeed extremely fertile.

BOTH SIDES OF my paternal great-grandparents came into this land during its first years of production. In 1857 my great grandfather Apperson's family traveled the first leg of the Oregon Trail from their original home in southern Illinois. Francis Apperson's wife had been dead seven years, possibly in childbirth with my great-grandfather, James Kimble Apperson, who was just seven years old when his father decided to first search for gold in the hills of California. If unsuccessful, they could return to their standby, farming. Leaving their greener home behind, James Kimble, his father and older brother and sister, traversed the plains following along the Platte River.

It was a rugged crossing that many would not survive. Thousands were left buried in unmarked graves along the trail's path. Sadly, the same fate would befall James Kimble's nine-year-old sister, Sarah. The child's father and brothers buried her somewhere along the Snake River. They could do nothing but continue on to California. Once in present southern Idaho the Oregon Trail was left behind as the family took the California Trail across the lengthy and dry desert and headed into the steep rise of the Sierra. They crossed the Donner Pass in 1857, a decade after the tragic Donner Party, and settled near Mariposa, in gold country. While making unsuccessful attempts at mining they planted an apple orchard which sustained them. At picking time they piled their crop onto their buckboard and traveled down into the San Joaquin Valley to market where they must have seen the stability of farmland. Although they held on to the Mariposa property on what is still named Apperson Mine Road and are documented as owning a cattle ranch in the Cholame Valley of the Coast Range Mountains, it was the 120 acres located northeast of Tulare Lake which grounded them. They established themselves as vineyardists in 1869. It was here that my great-grandfather married, and my grandfather Carl Apperson, and his three brothers were born.

James Kimble's eventual in-laws, the Watts, came by a similar route. John Watts was born in North Carolina and moved with his parents to Kentucky when he was still a child. After serving in the Revolutionary War, he returned to a life of farming in Kentucky and married Elizabeth Ewing Berry Yocum. After the birth of Margaret, my great-great grandmother, they moved to Missouri where John entered an ill-fated run at the state legislature. When he heard of gold discovery in California, he invested in cattle with the help of some financial partners and headed west. John was 61. He left behind his wife, teenage children, Margaret and her younger brother Jack, and many older children from his and Elizabeth's blended family. The Watts Party took the Santa Fe Trail which followed the Rio Grande River south to the beginning of the Old Spanish Trail that entered in southern California. After a short stay in Cold Springs, he also settled in Mariposa where John became Justice of the Peace. Although he traveled back to Missouri to bring his wife and sons to Mariposa in 1852, Margaret would have to wait over two decades before she was able to see California.

After settling her husband's estate after his death in the Civil War, and having collected enough from her parents' and brothers' mining efforts, Margaret booked a car on the first transcontinental train in 1872. She homesteaded land in the Hanford-Armona region the next year. Eventually, together with her daughter Elfleda, my great-grandmother, and Elfleda's husband, James Kimble Apperson, and his family, they established the Contact Mining and Milling Company in Mariposa.

My grandmother's father's family experienced a kindred journey. Henry Beaver, my grandmother's grandfather, made two trips across the Oregon/California Trails prior to making his final move to Santa Rosa in 1853. In 1849, he too tried his luck in the gold mines, traveling to the state with the Hudspeth-Myers party. Less than six months later, and nearly penniless, he returned to his wife and family in Missouri via a Nicaraguan passage. Although this left his family near financial ruin, he held the dream of the promised land of California. A year later, in 1851, Henry tried his hand at driving sheep to California after realizing feeding his fellow weary miners could be a prosperous venture. Unfortunately, this too was unsuccessful, the sheep dying in route. Henry turned back halfway to his destination. On his third and final crossing to California he gambled all and brought his family consisting of his wife, Lurana Cockrill Beaver, their children, several of her siblings and their families, along with numerous cousins. In some instances, there were four generations from a family traveling together. One of the cousins, William H. Zilhart, known in family records as a "semi-literate cowhand," recorded the voyage in his diary. He made nearly daily entries in what has become known as his *Ledger of My Travels from Missouri to California*. The Hagans-Cockrill wagon train, consisting of 125 people, left Pleasant Gap in western Missouri in April and arrived in California in October. The diary is filled with accounts of horse thievery, Indian encounters, driving hailstorms, and fights among the wagon party. On the date of June 11, 1853, Zilhart gives us a visual of the numbers of people heading west:

> We traveled about six miles to Laramie Fork. There were so many wagons there we could not cross until next day yesterday the boat sunk with several mean [sic] and women in it, but there were no lives lost today. The boat sunk with some stock and some men. They all got out safe. We camped on the bank of the river,

there was five hundred wagons there waiting
to cross.

Once in California, Henry and his extended family settled in Santa Rosa where he continued to be unsuccessful in most of what he tried. He was a brick maker by trade and was able to build a stately brick Classic Revival home known ever after as the Beaver House, even though Henry lost his home and brick yard with "200,000 well-burnt brick" and 150 acre ranch to a sheriff's sale in 1857. He could not re-pay the $1,500 mortgage he took out against the home in order to help build a school, among other establishments, in his growing community. Located on Beaver Street, it suffered damage in the 1969 earthquake and was eventually torn down.

For a time, Henry worked for Henry Miller of the prosperous Miller and Lux cattle operation, the largest in the world at that time, before leaving this area for yet another fresh start in the San Joaquin Valley. This was the family's move to Lemoore where they would try their hand at farming once again.

Yet another epic journey to California was the O'Connor family's venture from Quebec around Cape Horn in 1852 when great-grandmother, Kate, was four-years-old. Although the journey was vastly different, it was no less perilous.

She eventually met and married my great-grandfather, James Beaver, who was Henry Beaver's son. Together Kate and James, more successful with his endeavors than his father had been, accumulated a considerable amount of acreage and status in the area raising sheep. Therefore, one can only speculate as to why James and Kate left with Henry for the San Joaquin Valley. The likeliest reason was the sudden fall in demand for meat due to the diminishing number of miners and offers of more acres of virgin homestead land which they could call their own. And so they moved to the San Joaquin Valley to raise a crop and give birth to their family, with my grandmother, Genevieve Beaver, the youngest of eight, born in 1888.

These families marked a path that so many followed into the next century. They came for the proven fertile land and for its never-ending supply of water. But as the water kept its promise, the landscape altered dramatically and became a poor resemblance of its former existence.

When my ancestors first arrived in the San Joaquin Valley, the landscape, except for want of wildlife, still looked much as it had for centuries. The foliage that had changed due to overgrazing was not evident to the newcomers' eyes. They still saw a large amount of grassy plains although the native grasses had begun to be destroyed. Vernal pools formed in the small, mostly unnoticeable, depressions across the valley floor. Collecting water during the cooler months, the flowers at the edges changed depending on the amount of rainfall. Isolated oaks still spread far into a glistening horizon. This was wild landscape to them. These settlers sped the pace of change, altering the view for future generations. A patchwork spread over the once sprawling canvas of the valley floor. Lines began to stitch their way onto the frontier as acreage, roads, and communities created a new pattern on the land.

By the time of my family's arrivals in the valley, wheat constituted over ninety percent of the basin's cropland. Yet, alfalfa was soon found to grow well in the naturally alkali soil where the wheat, without proper fertilization, was quickly farmed-out. Due to the area's growing sheep ranching population in the Mussel Slough region, alfalfa became equal in numbers to wheat. This was also known as the Lucerne district because of its dairies situated along with the irrigated alfalfa fields.

My grandmother's family's eighty acres of alfalfa were situated in present Lemoore, which at the time of their move was, in wet years, located close to Tulare Lake's north shore, the edge of a region fondly known to early settlers as Tulare Valley. This was the amount of land provided under the Homestead Act. Once three years of residence was past, full ownership was granted to the settler. Great amounts of this area were homesteaded. In just one generation this town became, thanks to the introduction of the railroads, the nation's largest wool shipping point. The valley was quickly proving itself as an economic threshold. But, where commerce would escalate, frontier would subside.

At the time of their arrival the supply of water for the lake was so great that Tulare was known as the largest fresh water lake west of the Mississippi. Waters from not only the Kings, but Kern, Tule, and White rivers swelled the lake into a marshy, swamp-like haven for innumerable species of animals. Although hunting and trapping by this time was a bygone trade, fishermen could still fill their horse-drawn seines until their nets nearly exploded with fish. Anywhere from four to eight tons of fish caught in these seines could be taken in one haul.

Before the practice of cutting trees in the Sierra the large numbers of pines would slow the fast melting of snow and therefore the rivers that passed through the valley stayed fuller longer. This volume of water made navigation on these waterways possible. Navigation on the rivers, as well as the lake, had been important for both commerce and communication. In the southern region of the lake, the schooner, "Mose Andross," is recorded to have transported hogs and cattle from Atwell Island (now the town of Alpaugh) to destinations around the lake—Atwell's Landing on the north shore, Root Island on the south, and Gordon's Point in the west. The Water Witch was the most well-known boat on the lake both for its massive trappings of terrapin, which were transported to San Francisco for use in soups and stews, and for its original life as The Alcatraz, a dispatch boat between San Francisco and Alcatraz Island. In addition to these schooners, it is rumored that steamers on the Kings and the lake took passengers, as well as freight, to the growing number of settlements and inklings of new towns. While my grandmother's uncle, John, became a barge navigator on the lake and hauled lumber from Johnsondale, a large lumber mill site in the Sierra on the turbulent Kern River, the supply of good lumber in demand as the building of farm houses, tank houses, barns, and businesses in the valley grew, another Uncle, Oscar, became an established saloon keeper and farmer, cultivating 460 acres. Oscar made a good living in his new home, at least until he was killed by area train robbers, Sontag and Evans. He had joined the posse in hopes of earning the ten-dollar and oyster dinner reward. After a lengthy standoff, the posse charged the duo while holding up boards to block the assail of bullets. Oscar, unfortunately, threw down his board, his judgment blurred by drunkenness.

In a few years' time the lake had diminished substantially as many more settlers began diverting water and transforming this once swampy land into cultivated fields. The rivers began to stop short of their original destinations. This seed of change was actually planted in 1852 with the passage of the Swamp and Overflowed Lands Act. Once townships began to form, levees were built to protect them. Besides, the railroads that crossed the valley floor had taken over as a better form of moving people and produce around. At one point, the now small town of Goshen, 20 miles east of the lake, depending on the wetness of the year, had more trains passing through than there were entering New York's Central Station. Travel became exclusive to the land, and water vessels grounded themselves at the waters' edge.

As their ancestors had done in Missouri and Illinois, settlers' investments in their futures depended on the land. Lives were based on the soil, weather, and water and what they could make the land do for them. Cronise advised, ". . . it is in the power of those who choose, to attach their families to their homes, and give them a settled and contented feeling, which the immigrant should study to cultivate. In no other country are the elements so favorable to them in this respect."

These contented feelings created a newly felt attachment to the land. Communities had formed and with them a sense of belonging and commonality. Together, the community built schools and churches, and celebrated and mourned as one. This connection kept them focused on their dreams of shaping the frontier by working the land into perfectly square fields. It was at this time that my great-grandparents, James and Kate Beaver, and other citizens of their small town created the red and white quilt suggesting this connection. Scattered farming families gathered at town socials where there was a sense of fruition and endurance. Wallace Smith draws a picture of the time:

> . . . when youth gathered at a large home of
> a bonanza wheat grower, a rollicking fiddler
> was always present to furnish the music as the
> young men and women danced the polka,

waltz, schottische, mazurka, quadrille, or
the Virginia reel. Happy hearts vibrated in
complete harmony with the soothing landscape
which surrounded them.

My grandfather, Carl, was one of those fiddlers who
entertained audiences at town dances. He was a self-taught
musician who also played the violin, clarinet, flute, and
saxophone. In the earliest of photos, he stands in white
band uniform and hat, frog buttons being the only
ornamentation on an otherwise ordinary coat. He holds a
piccolo, a piece of sheet music clamped to its side. He is
fifteen, but looks much younger. The uniform obviously
too large for him, his arms are almost lost in the sleeves.
Always clean-shaven, his face is full, like that of a child. In
another photo taken five years later, he wears what appears
to be the same uniform. It fits him now. His hair is parted
in the middle, curls circling inward resting gently on his
forehead. His face has kept its softness. In this photo a
friend stands with him, an American flag between them.
"4th of July" is written on the back. In other photos he is a
part of the Farren Trio. Again in turn-of-the-century band
uniform, Grandpa holds a flute, another man a saxophone,
and a third, in hobo-character complete with a fake wooly
beard, torn clothes, and stove-pipe hat, plays a cello made
of a large metal can and broom. Still more photos are of
entire community bands with over a dozen members each.
In each of these Grandpa has a saxophone.

It was before one of these dances, a Fourth of July
celebration in 1905, where he and my grandmother first
met. From that night on, Grandma traveled with him to
each small town where he played. She saved all the dance
cards from these gatherings and stuck them between the

now brittle pages of her photo album. Although a few of the dances were taken up with a friend or two, the cards show, by the many blank spots, she mostly sat and listened to Grandpa's music.

Besides being a self-taught musician, my grandfather was also a self-taught artist. It is these traits that interested his grandfather's cousin, Phoebe Apperson Hearst. My grandfather's family routinely made trips by buckboard across the Coast Range Mountains, where they once owned a ranch in Bear Valley within the larger Cholame Valley, to camp at San Simeon with Phoebe. Phoebe, the one responsible for her son, William Randolph Hearst's, love for art by taking him as a child on an around-the-world cultural-fest, saw in my grandfather a talent she could nurture both monetarily and intellectually, something his poor farming parents could not. She offered to take him in, give him formal training in both music and art, but his parents refused. He was needed to work on the farm, tending livestock, sowing fields, and helping his father in the family mine. In his sketchbook, which I now have, he has what appear to be exercises on perspective, some unflattering caricatures of neighbors, and detailed maps. The most poignant of these maps, to me, is his pencil-sketch of California, its most predominant feature being Tulare Lake. No doubt the year he drew the map, as a 12-year-old in 1897, the lake was flourishing. I have often wondered if Phoebe propagated Grandpa's dreamer qualities, filling his head with ambitions of an unburdened artistic life never to be realized.

THEIRS WAS THE first generation to leave the land. Grandma, being the youngest of a large family that included many brothers taking care of the farm, perhaps realized there was no future for her in the small town. With no prospects at the time of marrying my grandfather, she moved to Oakland and secretarial school just in time to watch San Francisco burn down from across the Bay. Just two years later, in 1908, James Beaver, my grandmother's father, died. Devastated by the loss of her husband, Kate left the ranch in the hands of her son, Steve, and moved to Oakland to be with my grandmother. During that same time, my grandfather also moved from his family's farm that had three other brothers to support. He became an electrician for Standard Oil during the rebuilding of San Francisco. Their reuniting was chance, and for the following generations luck. While Grandma was riding through the city on a horse-drawn taxi, electrical wires that my grandfather was installing fell from his hands onto the seat next to her. Grandpa's once again slippery fingers led to their marriage in August of 1908.

8

It has been theirs to subdue the wilderness, and change it into smiling fields of bright growing grain.

—History of Tulare County, California

DISGRUNTLED MINERS WHO did not turn to cattle ranching took advantage of the valley's latest product, wheat—the dawning crop of the San Joaquin Valley. The price of flour in the mining towns was astronomical. At one dollar per pint, this was higher than the typical miner was earning if he were finding gold. They could make more money harvesting than gold panning. While much vegetation was introduced into the area accidentally, some of it was intentional. Upon seeing the productivity of the European grasses in the valley, settlers began planting field grains. Wheat harvesting became so successful that by the mid-1870s California was the number one state in the country for amount of wheat produced.

The main reason the valley found such prosperity with this crop was the expansion of the railways. Livestock could be shipped anywhere, and the speculation of raising crops became a reality because there was suddenly an accessible market which went beyond the mining towns and the state's borders. In the early 1870s rails began spreading over the entire valley. As with other progress, the end result was unavoidable alteration. The powering of the train engines, for one, was dependent upon the introduced Eucalyptus trees that remain numerous along freeways and in parks today. The change which arose due to the web of rail lines across the valley floor was as abundant as the lines themselves. The lumber that was so difficult to come by on the valley floor was shipped in from the north along with many comforts of everyday life that had been missing up to this point. Apparel and toiletries, books and musical instruments, were now obtainable in greater quantities. New dwellings sprung up across the landscape, with all the appropriate amenities such as parlors to accommodate settees and pianos. In agriculture, new varieties of wheat were available from other countries, and new experimentation began, with not only wheat but all types of produce, fruit and nuts being of growing interest.

Beyond creating access to markets across the country and world, this weave of rails created new townships across the mostly still-barren plain. Strategically-placed settlements, which began with water and loading stations, were plotted every five to seven miles along the lines. It was a mathematically constructed design laid out by the Southern Pacific railroad. William Preston illustrates this in his book *Vanishing Landscapes: Land and Life of the Tulare Lake Basin*:

> Nearly all Central Valley railroad towns shared a set of common features: centrality, accessibility from railroad grants, and a uniform plat. Smooth transfer of lots was ensured by the

adoption of a uniform plat, a rectangular grid aligned with the tracks rather than with the cardinal directions. Blocks were 400 feet by 320 feet, divided into thirty-two lots, and had axial alleys 20 feet wide. Residential streets were 80 feet wide, and major commercial arteries were 100 feet across. Uniformity was carried through the naming of streets: alphabetical names (A through Z Street) and California county names were preferred.

Virtually every town is similarly structured and has retained its Fresno, Tulare, Mariposa, and Merced streets.

Where mail stops once existed, opportune towns sprang up over night. This not only meant money for the ranchers and early farmers, but began openings for settlers who, for the first time, were dependent on commerce, not only the soil, for their livelihoods. Agricultural colonies, settlements consisting of small acreage farmers, formed because of both the emergence of the railroad and the newly implemented irrigation systems. Large landowners, upon seeing what profits selling or leasing land could bring, divided their land to settlers who often had migrated together and built new communities upon their arrival. Swedes established Kingsburg, German Mennonites in Reedley, a large Portuguese population in Hanford. Evidence of this can still be seen in the list of surnames in each community's directory.

The wheat farming days of the San Joaquin Valley, which lasted to the turn of the century, were known as the best of times. The landscape was perfect for the crop. The ground was flat and lacked obstacles such as numerous trees and rocks which could have hindered plowing. Summers were dry while the water of spring flowed plentifully in the rivers. Acreage was inexpensive with the only true investments being seed, a plow, and a few horses or oxen. Once the harvesting was done in the late summer and early autumn, it wasn't until the first part of the year before plowing and seeding was begun for the next harvest.

Life for the settlers was good but not always just. If land was not bought outright or homesteaded, many wheat farmers turned to squatting. The railroad opened its land to squatters who would settle the acreage with the intentions of later purchasing it from the railroad. The settlers assumed they would eventually buy the land from the railroad at cheap government rates, just as the railroad had. Once the railroad saw what improvements the settlers had made with their land, the railroad demanded high prices at selling time. This conflict, coupled with other problems between the settlers and the railroad, led to the Mussel Slough Tragedy of 1880, a gun battle near Hanford which left eight men dead. The fight and the circumstances leading up to this incident inspired Frank Norris to write his novel, *The Octopus.* In this novel the railroad takes a metaphorical form of an encompassing and sinister serpent.

> . . . the galloping monster, the terror of steel and steam, with its eye, cyclopean, red, shooting from horizon to horizon . . . the symbol of a vast power, huge, terrible, flinging the echo of its thunder over its path; the leviathan, with tentacles of steel clutching into the soil, the soulless Force, the iron-hearted Power, the monster, the Colossus, the Octopus.

The railroad affected almost every aspect of the valley's landscape. Towns which existed prior to railroad development, miles from the establishment of lines, were suddenly empty of people and commerce. Places such as Kingston, Cross Creek, and Clay Station are no longer evident on the valley floor. These three were passenger and supply stops along the Kings River leading toward Tulare Lake. Saloons, mail stops and stores were soon completely gone from the surface. Not even foundations remain where these early communities once bustled.

As economies changed, the agricultural colonies too began to break apart. Forty acres were no longer enough to keep a family fed. These communities also vanished from the valley floor. At times it was not only the settlers who suffered, but the land as well. Too often, settlers whose pasts in the gold mines had shown their desire for a quick dollar abused their soil, taking all the rich earth could give, but putting nothing back in return. Norris, again, writes:

> They had no love for their land. They were not attached to the soil. They worked their ranches as a quarter of a century before they had worked their mines. To husband the resources of their marvelous San Joaquin, they considered niggardly, petty, Hebraic. To get all there was out of the land, to squeeze it dry, to exhaust it, seemed their policy. When, at last, the land worn out, would refuse to yield, they would invest their money in something else; by then, they would have made fortunes. They did not care.

The wheat farmers not only damaged the soil due to a lack of crop rotation and fallowing, along with cattle and sheep ranchers that came before, they introduced more plants including noxious weeds into the region via new seed from other parts of the world. Although the days of wheat farming and sheep and cattle ranching are long past, their menaces are lasting reminders of their presence in the valley. The native perennial grasses were replaced by annual grasses due to the first Spanish missionaries who needed forage grass for their cattle. Bermuda grass came from Spain. It was under control until the valley began to see irrigation and intensive cultivation. The grass is now everywhere across the valley floor. Tumble weeds that now roll their way through the San Joaquin Valley are not an indigenous plant. They came from Russia. The main irritant to any cyclist on the valley's roads today is the puncture vine. It was brought to Tulare County when a wheat farmer imported several bags of white wheat seed, the most popular wheat for growing in the valley, from Australia. Harvest after harvest, the needle-like vine would come up, but never beyond his farm. That was until the invention of the automobile and its pneumatic tires which spread the vine throughout the valley. Only five percent of native grasses can be spotted among these nonnative plants today, and to control all growth, native and nonnative plants are sprayed so that at times of the year the sides of the roads and the dying foliage are all an unearthly orange color.

Once farming began, the valley oak, the one steadfast against intrusion up to this time, was in peril. The random spacing of these imposing trees could not configure into the alignment of furrows. They were merely in the way of increasingly valuable cropland. Oaks, whose roots spread deep into the soil, were finally blasted out of the ground. Yet shade trees were still needed, especially when the wave of heat hit in the summer months. Other shade and ornamental trees were introduced. Pomegranates, a southwestern Asia native, and maples surrounded homes. Palms, a symbol of triumph, became fitting additions. Pampas grass, a South

American native, and pitahaya from the southwestern desert, among others, added to the landscape's altered appearance.

John Muir, known for his writings about the Sierra Nevada forests, and the person credited for the preservation of wilderness areas, wrote this about the valley in "The Bee-Pastures":

> When California was wild, it was one sweet bee-garden throughout its entire length, north and south, and all the way across from the snowy Sierra to the ocean . . . . But of late years plows and sheep have made sad havoc in these glorious pastures, destroying tens of thousands of the flowery acres like a fire, and banishing many species of the best honey-plants to rocky cliffs and fencecorners, while, on the other hand, cultivation thus far has given no adequate compensation, at least in kind . . . . The time will undoubtedly come when the entire area of this noble valley will be tilled like a garden, when the fertilizing waters of the mountains, now flowing to the sea, will be distributed to every acre, giving rise to prosperous towns, wealth, arts, etc. Then, I suppose, there will be few left, even among botanists, to deplore the vanished primeval flora. In the mean time, the pure waste going on—the wanton destruction of the innocents—is a sad sight to see, and the sun may well be pitied in being compelled to look on.

This new garden did come, in an abundance which Muir could not possibly envision.

9

During that short half-century the march of civilization had changed the frontier from a reality into a tradition; it had converted the waste places into populous cities and transformed cattle and sheep pastures into highly cultivated farms; it had subdued wilderness and planted an empire by the Western sea.

—Robert Cleland,
From Wilderness to Empire

DURING THE YEARS of the rise of agribusiness, in the first part of the 20th century, my father's family lived, for the most part, in the city. After their marriage in 1908, Grandma and Grandpa stayed in the Bay area for six more years, rearing their first two sons in Richmond. In 1914 they moved back to the valley, seeing another chance at an opportunity this region could offer. My grandfather and his brother, Uncle Bud, saw an enterprise in all the electric-powered water pumps being established in the still-developing farmland. Their electrical business had no store-front at first as they remained outdoors in the fields working for one farmer to the next. As their business quickly grew, they did open a store with lighting fixtures, eventually expanding to have refrigerators in their stock. Their prosperity was short-lived. My grandfather was no businessman. He let customers, such as the county's district attorney for one, take refrigerators without paying up front, and then was never able to collect the debt. Before long he was bankrupt and by then had two more sons to feed.

They left the San Joaquin Valley and moved to Los Angeles where they raised an eventual seven children in the noise and commotion of the sprawling city. This was for them another promising future. Although there was a great deal of farming in Los Angeles at the time, there were industries and ports full of jobs to be had. They first moved to 23rd Street and then to Georgia Street in downtown where my grandmother's sister, Lorraine, had a boarding house.

Lorraine was the industrious one, independent and self-reliant. She was the first in her family to leave the ranch and attended Woodbury Business College in Los Angeles. Thirteen years my grandmother's senior, Lorraine must have been a role model for her. She was a striking woman who loved to have her photo taken. In one series of photos, late in her life, her auburn and gray hair is pulled loosely atop of her head, a few wisps of wiry strands fall, defying the restraint. A silk wrap embraces her bare shoulders and she wears a large sterling crucifix around her neck. There is always a faint smile and certain strength in her almond-shaped eyes. Other candid photos have her sitting casually in a long white dress with a high buttoned collar, hair upswept, as usual. A large photo of herself is displayed on the upright piano at which she sits. She became the matriarch of the family.

Grandpa either did not find work or was disillusioned with the available jobs. Perhaps he was not cut out for the conventional. He hooked rugs for a while, something with which he could be creative, but his family suffered. Their troubles compounded.

A few days before Christmas in 1924, Billy, the youngest of four boys at the time, stood in their kitchen begging my grandmother to let him open his one Christmas present early. She refused and, after so much pleading, ordered the five-year-old outside to play with his brothers. He left in tears. His brothers were across the street calling him over when he ran out into the road and in front of a car. He died instantly. "If I had only let him have his present . . . ," my grandmother cried until the final days of her life. My grandmother said that if she had not been pregnant with her next son, she simply would not have lived. She would go on to have her only daughter, and one final son, my father. One year after my father was born, the Depression hit. Life in their household only became more dire, and the family became even more dependent on Aunt Lorraine who by this time had married Dr. Bailey, an optometrist.

GRANDPA, ALWAYS THE dreamer, still had hopes of finding riches on Apperson Ridge in the hills above the Kings River or north from there, in Mariposa, on the land where his great-grandfather Watts had first settled in 1849. My grandfather's parents still lived in Mariposa, my great-grandfather continuing his gold-mining. Somehow he talked my grandmother into returning to the valley one more time. She disliked the mountains, always referring to them as "those hot hills." One of her first experiences traveling to the mine was when she was in the last months of pregnancy with her first child. It was August of 1909 when she road a buckboard from where they mined across the valley to the family ranch in Lemoore. The trip took twelve hours. An old and dying miner, needing the attention of a doctor, lay in the buckboard behind where she and her driver sat, his moans lasting the duration of the trip. It reached 100 degrees, and she was miserable. My grandfather's mining would remain a contention between them throughout their marriage.

Nevertheless, in 1934, my grandmother agreed to return to his mine as long as she and the children could live in the city. Merced was the largest valley town closest to Mariposa, and so this is where they settled. Some of my father's earliest recollections were of living in Merced and their trips up the hill to Mariposa. They were both his fondest and most despised of memories. Only knowing downtown Los Angeles up to that point, he loved the openness and wild of the mountains. However, without a steady income, the family continued their reliance on Relief. Living directly behind the Tioga Hotel my father, along with his older brother and sister, would stand in the alley behind the hotel with pails in hand asking the kitchen crew for the discards. Less than one year later, with the mine as penniless as ever, they returned to Los Angeles and the support of Aunt Lorraine.

BY THE TIME my father came back to the land 35 years later, yet one more aspect of the landscape had transformed. The Kings River, which used to flow by its own free will, now has five reservoirs, eighteen small dams, or weirs, and sixty-one diversions to irrigate crops. Fields of natural grasses, numerous oak trees following the Kings River across the plain, an array of wild game in the air, waters, and fields, have been almost completely erased from the valley's surface. Today there are crops instead of grasses, irrigation canals instead of sloughs, and rails, roads, and housing subdivisions across the human-populated floor. A new pattern has unfolded across the landscape.

Elemental to this, the controversial Central Valley Water Project, approved by President Roosevelt in 1935, created one of the largest water systems on earth. Originally designed to promote the small farmer in irrigating his 160 acres or less, it was repealed in 1982 so that large, some corporate, farms of up to 960 acres could be irrigated. What was realized was a massive water system which many point to as the means of environmental ruin. The main purpose of the Pine Flat Dam on the Kings River was to keep waters from reaching Tulare Lake, making the area available for farming.

There were nearly one million prong-horned antelope and half as many tule elk in the valley when Grizzly Adams and his contemporaries arrived. They were all but gone by the 1920s at the hands of hunters and farmers alike. The fragile new shoots of alfalfa or tree fruit were new food for rodents on which Red-tailed hawks, peregrine falcon, and owls fed. Jackrabbit and ground squirrel drives utilizing both guns and dogs took down hundreds of the animals in each hunt. Frank Norris captures such a scene,

> The earth was alive with rabbits . . . . Then the strange scene defined itself. It was no longer a herd covering the earth. It was a sea, whipped into confusion, tossing incessantly, leaping, falling, agitated by unseen forces. At times the unexpected tameness of the rabbits all at once vanished. Throughout certain portions of the herd eddies of terror abruptly burst forth. A panic spread; then there would ensue a blind,

> wild rushing together of thousands of crowded
> bodies, and a furious scrambling over backs;
> till the scuffing thud of innumerable feet over
> the earth rose to a reverberating murmur as of
> distant thunder, here and there pierced by the
> strange, wild cry of the rabbit in distress . . . .
> The noise made by the tens of thousands of
> moving bodies was as the noise of wind in
> a forest, while from the hot and sweating
> mass there rose a strange odor, penetrating,
> ammoniacal, savouring of wild life. On signal,
> the killing began.

IN SPITE OF all these changes to the valley's floor, a person looking at a map of the San Joaquin Valley, such as the one on the wall of the St. Louis museum, will see a smooth green valley. There are no implications of the miles of grid-patterned design consisting of barren canal banks and crop rows. They will not see the orange-colored roadsides full of dying plants, the absence of oak trees, or lack of native fauna. A topographical map such as this would virtually look the same as a map designed over one hundred years ago when the landscape was in its natural state. Only one difference would be seen between the two, Tulare Lake.

Its 700 square miles of surface at one time covered a noticeably large section on the maps. Today it is usually unacknowledged with only a few maps faintly positioning the Tulare Lake Basin region. The waters of the Kings River, along with the Kern, White, and Tule, no longer complete their run to its shores. They are halted miles away as they now feed furrowed land.

Although the lake was, in great areas, only a foot deep, the middle of the lake was over forty feet in depth. Because the lake could go from 195 square miles, at its lowest, to 760 square miles, at its highest, many speculated that there was a subterranean passage from the lake to the ocean causing the escape of waters. However, this change in water level was merely evaporation caused by the summer's sweltering heat. It would take much more to drain the lake entirely.

In a local newspaper article of June, 1898, it was reported, "'Tulare Lake is drying up. Its waters are constantly receding. Like the dawning of a new creation pleasant groves and fertile fields take the place of its former wastes of waters.'" Two months later, an article in the same newspaper was more melancholy in tone.

> Tulare Lake is dry as a chip. For the first time in recent history the pelican geese, ducks, snipes, mudhens, and other birds, as well as the finny fish, have found that there is no longer a home for them in the biggest pond of fresh water this side of the Rocky Mountains . . . . Year after year the inroads made by man have encroached upon its wide expanse and where the angular crane once fished for suckers among the tules, and the wild geese, ducks and the majestic swan dwelt in peace and plenty, the horny-handed wheat grower is sacking up 12 to 15 sacks of Sonora wheat to the acre.

In irregularly wet years the lake would once again fill, but there are very few existing photographs of this to show the citizens of the valley what a grand natural habitat used to be here. Picture an ocean, smooth and silent into the curved horizon. Drawings from over a century ago show large schooners skirting the shores to destinations such as

Terrapin Bay, Atwell's Island, and Gordon's Point. The lake, however, was not always so serene. Sudden and sometimes rough storms fell upon it from the northwest making navigation difficult and causing several shipwrecks. The following is an account of such a storm by a sailor on the Water Witch:

> Part of the time we flew before the wind, at a rate of eight or ten miles an hour, then the wind would lull and our speed would slacken a little. Part of the time the Water Witch kept ahead of the heaviest wind. Then came a lull, but soon the wind would catch us again, and away we went, dancing merrily over the troubled waters. It was splendid, exhilarating. Once in a while a larger wave than usual would dash over our sides, and many a time the boom of the mainsail dipped to leeward in the waves . . . .

The Water Witch, which was launched from the Kings River twenty miles before the lake, finally wrecked just three miles southeast of the mouth of the river.

There exist only two known photographs of the lake. Both are sepia panoramas. In one, a group of four men sit two abreast in a long, narrow boat. Although they are in the foreground of the scene, their faces are difficult to discern. They are looking down, perhaps busying themselves with preparations to fish, the wide brims of their hats cast shadows, hiding their faces even more. The end of the boat points toward the seemingly endless lake. The sun shines through a break in an overcast sky, casting ripples of reflected sunlight beside the boat. There are no features in the horizon, only the water rounding its way out of sight.

The second photograph shows the same four men, not exactly posing, in front of a crudely pitched canvas tent and windbreak on what looks like a muddy peninsula, again the lake's water surrounding the men. The row boat pictured in the first photograph rests lengthwise to the left of the frame. The sun barely forces its way through the gloomy sky.

The fact that there are only these two found photographs of Tulare Lake is symbolic in that this place, this once enormous physical feature, arguably mythical in its size, has nearly vanished from our visual record as well.

PATHS CROSS OFTEN from generation to generation, especially when a family lives in a region over a span of one hundred years or more. After my sister, Kim, graduated from college with a degree in fisheries biology, she worked for a time as a private consultant. One job led her to what was left of Tulare Lake. In the fall of 1983 through the summer of 1984, the year of El Niño and the heavy rains it brought, Tulare Lake was beyond the capacity of its man-made borders. Still only at one quarter of its original capacity, it flooded acres of the corporate farming land of Salyer and Boswell, transforming it into twenty feet of muck. Eager to have this portion of land back into production, they wanted to pump water from the lake into the San Joaquin River system. However, the fear was that the white bass which existed in Tulare Lake would get into the San Joaquin, compete with its natural salmon and striped bass, and eventually ruin fishing in the Delta, a large industry. The Tulare Reclamation District hired my sister to collect data on the white bass in the lake and research their spawning history. During her fieldwork, she boated beside corrugated shed roofs and road signs, their tops just above water level. Waterfowl had returned and the fish population exploded in the succulent, drowned farmland. For a brief time the lake reclaimed some of its grandeur.

The lake was eventually sprayed with rotenone not long after she left, poisoning all wildlife existing there. Later that year this mighty corporate farm, which after so much wheeling and dealing to get its land back into production, was subsidized by the government to not plant crops.

MY FATHER JOINED me one spring Sunday morning in my sudden determination to find Tulare Lake, and a remnant of what this region of the valley once resembled. We tried to follow the course of the Kings River from near our farm to the lake. It is a green oasis as it winds its way through the valley, from Piedra near Pine Flat Dam on down to the Lemoore area. The river breaks up the mundane configuration of the valley with its uniform rows of fruit trees, grapevines, and parallel roads. The often dry river bottom sinks and rises, oaks stand majestic, and roads we traveled dead-ended or were forced to make turns. The closer Dad and I ventured toward the lake, the more this setting changed. The farther south the darker, and richer, the soil. A maze of large canals divide the land which at the time was freshly plowed, no crops, no buildings, no homes, nothing, just bare opaque ground into the wavering horizon.

By process of elimination we found the road to what would have been near the center lake and ignored the "No Trespassing" sign of a corporate farm. The dirt road we were on was like so many others in the vicinity. It doubled as a levee. A wide, swift canal ran on one side of this road which sat far above the cultivated land. A man discing a field waved. With some hesitation we waved back, hoping our pickup truck would make us inconspicuous. Still miles from the lake, a mirage formed making the distance shimmer an eerie reflection of lifelessness. "Surreal," my father said after miles of silence. Finally one waving illusion transformed into water. Six massive rectangle holding ponds were broken up by yet more levees. The earth at the edges of the water is white from salinization which is a concern for much of the soil in this southeastern region. The land here looks as if it were dusted with snow, a problem caused when irrigated water and the natural Corcoran clay soil mix. The land is no longer viable. Birds which try to reproduce here often have offspring with deformities know as "Kesterson Syndrome." I walked to the caked edge and stood amazed at what a once vast lake had become. Immediately south of what is left of the lake is a wide stretch of unplanted soil. Unplowed, I could now visualize what this region resembled at the time this lake was in its greatness. Tall shoots of tules covered the open ground. Short grasses were sprung up between the tules, leaving me to wonder if these were some of the bunchgrasses I had read of but had never seen. A Phoebe bird landed ever-so gently on the end of a tule, making it bow slightly. I wanted to stay, watch for wildlife, fast-forward to see how the plant-life and colors changed with each season, as I had also read.

I imagined my grandparents on buckboard traversing this plain, coming to the edge of the lake, and pausing there with me.

10

'The wilderness, and the solitary place shall be glad for them; and the desert shall rejoice, and blossom as the rose.'

—Wallace Smith,
Garden of the Sun

DISCRETION FACTORS HEAVILY when it comes to the concerns of land ownership and treatment. A balance regarding ownership and a justification of treatment is reached to fit our own desires. The changes to the landscape my family has witnessed over the generations have much to do with the river which we have depended on for our livelihoods. Since the beginning of human intervention, the river, like the land, has been altered dramatically.

The early farmers moved to what they could afford. Mostly disappointed gold miners, they found the land cheap but more promising than the gold which was then California's most valuable natural resource. As more and more land was settled, the fight over water rights began. Water quickly surpassed gold, becoming California's most valuable resource in the twentieth century. The lesson was learned early on—that which is most valuable is used to its greatest extent.

"The time will come when irrigation, as a grand system, will be called for and adopted, rendering the more extensive culture of these articles probable," forecast Titus Cronise in 1868. The system would become grander than anything he could have imagined.

The evolution of irrigation closely followed the evolution of land use in the valley. At the time Cronise predicted the use of water in the valley, some small gravity water diversions were already in use for livestock in isolated areas. Soon, with the emergence of wheat farming, water from the river was transported into more acreage, and the potential was seen for the ability to raise more diverse crops. In looking at an oak's growth rings the diversion of the waters is apparent. The rings grow smaller beginning around 1855. By 1875 water was steadily taken into parched land by a growing number of canals and irrigation companies. For the most part, these were small farmers banding together in hopes of increasing their crop yields. Drought was the farmers' greatest fear, but possibly the most avoidable circumstance they faced. With the experience many of them had as miners, the crude early engineering was largely successful. The level landscape actually made the job easier. Natural sloughs and tributaries were merely deepened and widened.

Canal construction was a toilsome endeavor but a mere trifle of what it paid off. Slip scrapers used in the rock-filled earth of the eastern states were used at first to dig these channels, but they proved unworkable in the sandy loam soil of the valley. Wallace Smith describes the movement of earth:

> Each of them used a hundred teams. The slip scraper proved inefficient as it always did in this type of work. At first the ground was plowed deeply and Hawn then devised a buck scraper of wood, formed like a heavy drag, with runners at each end. Where the soil was moved down grade, this contrivance made it possible to move a yard of earth on each trip.

Soon the Fresno scraper, a modified version of the slip scraper, was built which not only worked in the region's soil but was sold around the world.

The fights over water rights and the number of agencies, state, federal, and private, began as soon as the first plow hit the valley's virgin soil. Two conflicting traditions concerning the rights of water existed in California at this time. These were the riparian rights, which derived from English law, and the idea of prior appropriation. Riparian rights not only restricted the landowner's use of stream-side water, it also halted those living nearby from using its waters if it might diminish its quality or quantity. This law worked well in the dampness of the east and in England where irrigation was not relied on. The arid land in the valley, however, was a new climate for raising crops. The miners, who had been in the state for some time, were accustomed to claiming water and directing its flow without concern for others downstream. The Wright Act of 1887 settled the controversy and, ultimately, changed the irrigation patterns of the valley. Whereas water and land had been considered separate entities, this act united the two. Water became accessible to all landowners' properties. Soon cooperative efforts constructed large irrigation networks, weirs, and levees.

By the turn of the 20th century, this valley area consisted of six irrigation districts, involving 500 miles of main canals, and nearly one million acres of productive land; 60,000 of these acres irrigated by the Kings River alone. The monetary value of the land increased with each diversion of water to it. Land that was once undesirable to new settlers due to its isolated location far from streams or the river was suddenly arable and much more valuable.

The sites of my ancestors' farms were not so lucky. Located far down the Kings River's path, the majority of its water was already diverted miles before reaching their point. What water they would take from the Tulare Lake was diminishing and of poor quality because the Kings and smaller rivers were no longer able to give their once abundant waters. Once again, the ex-miners' experience in using the land to work for them settled the problem. Well-drilling was easy in the natural alluvial soil and irrigation pumps (those which my grandfather worked on as an electrician) became the next landmark on the valley's landscape.

Wallace Smith wrote in 1939:

> At the present time the people of the San Joaquin Valley are conducting a great experiment in irrigation and intensive farming. Judging the future by the past, it may safely be assumed that they will encounter many fortunes but never that of defeat.

Today segments of the river's course are often drained dry, replaced by the angular veins of the valley's canal system. No other factor, trapping, cattle ranching, wheat farming, or the railroad, had a greater impact on the valley's landscape than irrigation.

MY OWN PERCEPTIONS about the use and conditions of this valley's landscape have been challenged, changed, and above all, perhaps, compromised over the years. With the Kings River a mile from my family's farm and no access to its banks without trespassing, the canal that ran across the street graduated in status to a natural place. As a child I came to treasure that canal and the semblance of nature it could support. In some years Mallard and Wood ducks made the canal their nesting ground, and if we kept a comfortable distance we could watch them swim up and down the thin waterway, ducklings in tow. On more than one morning, an egret appeared walking its careful yet deliberate pace along the far side of the canal and adjacent vineyard. Coyotes routinely trotted the banks, suspiciously stopping, looking around to determine the least noise. Then there was the rare volunteer oak tree that quickly grew out of the side of the canal almost as if it wanted to establish itself before the irrigation management workers could uproot it from the bank. One year, in anticipation of one such oak tree's removal, we dug it up ourselves transplanting it to my parents' yard where it is still thriving.

It was late one summer evening when I was walking my spirited German shepherd along the packed-down canal bank, its waters having passed in front of my parents' farm only minutes before. This canal, in the Consolidated Irrigation District, is the product of one of the first constructions which brought water from the Kings River. Today, 28 Kings River water agencies exist. This is the canal along the road which my mom used to drive me to school. On the east side of the road was this bank, looking much the same as it does today, hard-packed, sandy dirt sprayed with herbicides to deter plant growth. On the west side was a mile long stretch of plum orchards with only one crossroad and one old farmhouse interrupting their uniformity. Today the canal is the town's barrier, the only object blocking further growth. On the west side of this road is now a pricey subdivision and although it would be an easier walk on that side of the road with its wide smooth sidewalk and streetlamps to light our way, my dog and I walk the bumpy, dusty canal. We were nearer the frogs that way, a noise I have missed since moving away from my parents' farm and into town. Through a crack in my bedroom window, my sleepless summer nights were filled with the deep groans of frogs and baying of coyotes. Now I must seek them out.

I am grateful that this stretch of the canal has remained above ground. Further down the road, with the prospect of building new houses, the canal has been placed underground. It is also meant to save water from evaporation during the summertime months. As my dog and I reached the last few steps of the canal, we could see, due to the bright streetlights, the smooth dirt covering the underground canal as we heard the loudest chorus of frogs futilely searching for their watery home. But I miss the canal, the last refuge for so many animals; not just frogs but those ducks, egrets, and fish which survived the break-up of the river. Some citizens have purposely planted oaks, a scattering of California poppies, or a meandering rose from their garden hoping to beautify the barren canal banks. This is met with opposition as such plantings impede the routine scraping or weed abatement. The oak, it is claimed, takes too much of the valuable water if it were allowed to grow.

11

The Senator says the territory of California is three times greater than the average extent of the new States of the Union. Well, Sir, suppose it is. We all know it has three times as many mountains, inaccessible and rocky hills, and sandy wastes, as are possessed by any State of the Union. But how much is there of useful land? How much that may be made to contribute to the support of man and of society? These ought to be the questions. Well, with respect to that, I am sure that everybody has become satisfied that, although California may have a very great sea-board, and a large city or two, yet that the agricultural products of the whole surface now are not, and never will be, equal to one half part of those of the State of Illinois; no, nor yet a forth, or perhaps a tenth part.

—Daniel Webster, attributed

TO UNDERSTAND THIS region of the San Joaquin Valley it is necessary to first understand the water of the Kings River. The river feeds this valley, making it possible to claim it as the most productive farming area in the world, ever.

In all, farmers now utilize 3.2 million acre feet of water from the Kings River annually, irrigating over one million acres of agricultural land and producing three billion dollars worth of produce. This, combined with urban use, means that 87 percent of the King's flow is drained. The Kings River has won the distinction of being one of the largest rivers in the United States that is consumed so completely.

"In the vast Sierra wilderness far to the southward of the famous Yosemite Valley, there is a yet grander valley of the same kind," wrote John Muir in his 1891 essay, "A Rival of the Yosemite: The Canyon of the South Fork of Kings River, California." This grander valley cradles the Kings on its southern journey through Kings Canyon National Park until it joins the Middle Fork of the river at Yucca Point at the meeting of the Monarch Wilderness and the Sequoia and Sierra National Forests. Combined, the waters of the Kings River travel 16 miles until the river is halted at Pine Flat Reservoir.

To know the river is to appreciate the rugged canyons which it has formed. Some of the southernmost glaciers in America feed the headwaters of these two branches. The South Fork of the Kings River begins at 11,000 feet among glacial lakes and numerous granite peaks. For the 42 miles making its way to its convergence with the Middle Fork, the South Fork travels along the Pacific Crest National Trail, also known as the John Muir Trail. It rushes among alpine meadows and lakes, passing the dense forests at Cedar Grove. The river swiftly crashes upon the rugged surfaces until reaching the park boundary, where it then acts as a boundary between the Sequoia and Sierra National Forests. Boulder-induced rapids stir the water as it disappears from sight traveling under the steep canyon slopes. At 2,240 feet the Main Stem is created.

As with the South Fork, the Middle Fork also begins at more than 11,000 feet above sea level, traveling through meadows, granite walls and over a dozen waterfalls. In the most rugged of this stretch are six of these falls, making the river drop 320 feet a mile in one five mile long section. Paralleling the Middle Fork for 10.3 miles is once again the Pacific Crest Trail. Once passing Tehipite Valley, what many consider one of the most extraordinary sights in the Sierra, the Middle Fork reaches the western boundary of the Kings Canyon National Park. Eight rugged, and mostly inaccessible, miles later, the Middle Fork meets the South Fork, ending the Middle's 35 mile run.

The North Fork, which does not meet the waters of the Middle and South Forks until the short section between Rodgers Crossing and Pine Flat Reservoir, does not have so free a rein. On its equally long, and once picturesque, course it is halted by two dams plus numerous penstocks and tunnels.

The Main Stem of the Kings River then runs for 159 miles in its long stretch from the canyons of the Sierra to the parched San Joaquin Valley.

A naturally arid land, the San Joaquin Valley uses the waters of eight rivers flowing from the Sierra, from Stockton to Bakersfield. The Kings, however, was and continues to be the greatest supplier of water. It was in the early stages of agricultural production in this region that the necessity of controlling the river began. As Charles Kaupke, a former Water Master for the Kings River Water Association, wrote in *Forty Years on the Kings River*, "What the valley needed was men with vision and courage, and got them. These men put water to work." In 1954, nearly twenty years after

President Roosevelt signed the Central Valley Water Project, Pine Flat Reservoir was completed by the Army Corps of Engineers for irrigation, flood control, and to allow farming in the heart of Tulare Lake Basin. It is California's eleventh largest impoundment out of 1,300 major reservoirs. As it turns out, the Kings is one of the most extensively developed hydroelectric systems in the country. Pacific Gas and Electric's network of reservoirs, tunnels, penstocks, and powerhouses wills the water three times as it drops 7,000 feet in 20 miles.

FIFTY YEARS BEFORE the completion of the reservoir, my father's parents, and some of their relations, frequently traveled this area, going back and forth from their family farms to their land just above the drowned river. By buckboard they crossed nearly 50 miles of the valley, passed the natural and sparsely vegetated landscape and the plowed furrows of newly established farms to the foothills just below the present Pine Flat Reservoir. From there they rode alongside the river and through the small resort town of Trimmer, now all under one million acre feet of water. More prosperous than mining, tree felling was a large industry in the Sierra. My grandmother's friend, an exuberant and free-spirited woman, chose to ride the logging flume from Trimmer to the valley on their return trips.

One year before my grandmother, Genevieve, died my family piled into the car and drove along Trimmer Spring Road, turning off at Big Creek. At age ninety, Grandma wanted to see "Yoo Hoo" rock one more time. This is the rock she would climb to from the family camp below and yell "Yoo Hoo," the sound echoing through the small canyon and to my grandfather so that he would know supper was ready. It is an endearing story, because it is about the few times that they were together in the hills.

The area my grandfather tried to mine was Apperson Ridge. It now looks over one of the muddy spider-legged inlets of Pine Flat Dam at its most north east point. The ridge was named for my grandfather and great-grandfather who had ill-fated hopes of becoming rich on beryllium. It was located within part of the Watts Mining Claim owned by my great-grandfather's brother-in-law, Jack Watts. In 1888, over thirty-five years after arriving in Mariposa and mining Pea Ridge, Jack established his claim in this piece of the Sierra.

It didn't take many years for the area to change. At the time they tried to mine, my grandfather and great-grandfather and his brother-in-law saw no water from the Kings below the mountain. It was three miles off on the other side of Secata Ridge. Although we have a picture of my grandfather propping his eighty-seven-year-old body between the sign and his cane, the misspelled sign (it read "Appersen" instead of "Apperson") is now gone.

The Big Creek stream where they camped fed the Kings at one time and now feeds a reservoir. This stream acted as their link. The waters made their way from the hills just below Apperson Ridge and down to the valley floor. The river curved by its own volition through oak groves, riparian forests, and outlaying prairies which encompassed its shores until it made its way to Tulare Lake.

Whether my family was in the hills above the river, or using its water on their farms, they wielded nature to construct their livelihood. My own family's farm is located half way between my great-grandparents' farms and their property in the Sierra and just one mile from the Kings River. The tame canal that is across the road from the farmhouse has helped my family bring life to our farm. It becomes a balancing act as we place judgment on limits of the land's use. We are emotional about the land, whether it's our intention to use it or to keep it from further harm.

IN DRY YEARS, when the levels of the reservoir are low, the few remains of Trimmer are seen as foundations and chimneys reach out above the still water. They are remains of an era. As a child I stared at Yoo Hoo rock carefully to make an impression in my mind so that I could find it again on my own. But now, decades later, I cannot pick out Yoo Hoo from the other granite rocks which dot the hills. With the family sign now gone from the hill it too will become just one more ridge, its significance lost to our family history. My grandparents' own account of their voyages between the valley and hills, the stories and landscape they encountered, like the natural river here, are now gone among the years.

DURING THE TIME Native Americans alone lived on the valley floor, their density of population was correlated to the amount of second feet discharged by the stream by which they lived. Over the generations it has stayed much the same.

Rivers are life-giving features which turn arid dirt into verdant oases. This was true of the Tigris and Euphrates as they created the greatest farming region of the ancient world. And this is true of the Kings River which supplies the most productive farming area in the modern world. Rivers give wealth to those who use them most, who trap their waters and direct their flows.

"Nature makes huge demands, yet pays a thousand, thousand fold," wrote John Muir while trekking through the Kings River region. Today he might say that it is humans who make huge demands of nature, and we are paying a thousand, thousand fold.

12

And the owners not only did not work the farms any more, many of them had never seen the farms they owned.

—John Steinbeck,
The Grapes of Wrath

THERE ARE QUESTIONS that I keep asking myself. Is there a connection with the landscape when order is forced upon it? Does that act of organizing and controlling the land create the connection? Or does this act further pull us away emotionally? Emotions and land are viscerally tied, and yet I believe there are many who, working with land or not, do not sense this within themselves or have never asked these same questions. Can a connection to a place truly be made if you never live among and rely on it?

During the time that my grandparents did not live in this region, another significant change occurred. This was the emergence of corporate farming. It has an impact on not only the patterns of landscape but the towns and people in the area. Several contributing factors led to the growth of large scale farming. Early on, the state, in a hurry to get land in the hands of farmers and commerce, unloaded huge parcels at a time. The railroad then marketed these holdings at a great profit. As the next century began, the differences between these large farms and the small family farms became more distinct. Many situations, such as irrigation expenses, high land taxes, and the emergence of machinery use, added to this distinction, but perhaps the greatest cause came with the Great Depression. Small farms could no longer compete in global markets as prices fell. Large landowners could afford to drill down to water levels which had diminished substantially since the implementation of irrigation, a system the small farmers had begun.

Suddenly the landscape's old patterns of ownership were new again. Large land holdings filled the region, overtaking small plots. By mid-twentieth century almost sixty percent of the farm area of and around the reclaimed Tulare Lake consisted of farmland of one thousand acres or more. Populations, including whole towns, diminished because of the break-up of family farms when fewer people were needed to work these large parcels. The towns which remained suffered both socially and economically.

Although more than half of farms are 100 acres or less, like my family's, corporate ownership continues to grow. Studies have shown that towns consisting of lesser acreage farms fare well. Quality of life is high where people put money back into their communities. Successful schools and thriving neighborhoods are maintained. But the neglected towns depending on the corporate farms surrounding them rely on the seasonal population of migrant workers. No money is put back into a town where the farmer doesn't live. Schools are poor or nonexistent and housing is extremely depressed. Where there are no permanent crops, there are usually no permanent homes.

Unlike the small farmers who came to this region and created not only homes and towns, but an actual connection with the land on which they lived, farming corporations are run by individuals living hundreds of miles away, possibly who have never stepped foot on the valley's soil. Without this connection to the land, abuse is more prevalent. For the most part these are field crops, tomatoes and cotton predominately. Cotton especially consumes not only massive amounts of water but strips the land of its once rich elements.

The land is willed to produce by use of fertilizers, insecticides, and defoliants. Massive machinery cuts costs and new hybrid experimentation increases profits. Corporate farms have the revenue to put these products to work. The family farmer not only doesn't have the money for these implements but may be more conscientious when it comes to using substances such as herbicides and insecticides on their own property. It comes down to the connection, or lack thereof, that people have with the land. William Preston writes in *Vanishing Landscapes*, "Accompanying the loss of residual landscapes and places is a rapid erosion of the memories of the past, memories built by direct and intimate relationships with the land." Unlike the family farm, the corporate farm is not passed down from generation to generation and therefore familial roots are not given a chance to take hold.

The landscape differences between the two are apparent. Where small family-run farms contain signs of life the corporate farm is more "barren" than the early descriptions of the valley before settlers came to this wilderness. There is the sign of life in the green of crops planted but a lack of proof that people touch this ground. Buildings, for the most part, are missing from the landscape. There will always be that chance that another wet year will cause Tulare Lake to fill once again. What structures do exist are huge metal sheds, storage facilities for the array of farming implements. Without any signs of human presence, the viewer may see the landscape as a natural, peaceful setting; however, because of the presence of a few scattered buildings, we expect to see human life which is not there and presents a feeling of forsakenness.

John Steinbeck wrote in his epic 1939 novel primarily set in the valley, *The Grapes of Wrath*:

> And all the time the farms grew larger and the owners fewer. And there were pitifully few farmers on the land any more . . . . And it came about that the owners no longer worked on their farms. They farmed on paper; and they forgot the land, the smell, the feel of it, and remembered only that they owned it, remembered only what they gained and lost by it.

The prose is similar to Frank Norris' descriptions in *The Octopus* of the abandonment of the land at the hands of the wheat farmers. Comparable, too, are the accounts of hunters and trappers who took what they could out of the land and left. Decades after Steinbeck wrote these words, the situation is all the more widespread. The bonds which once tied farmers to not only their land but to their neighbors and communities as well will very likely never again contribute to quality of life in this region.

13

*Everywhere throughout the great San Joaquin,
unseen and unheard, a thousand ploughs
up-stirred the land, tens of thousands of shears
clutched deep into the warm, moist soil.*

—Frank Norris,
The Octopus

THE VALLEY HAS been accused of not having seasons. Spring and fall are short-lived, caught between the fog of winter and the heat of summer. But to anyone who lives here we see in the fields a definite change of seasons, from the snow-like layer of spring blossoms to the turning leaves of fruit trees which rival any New England color, to the starkness of winter's tule fog.

The final days of summer on my family's farm were the most distinct to me. While the mornings were beginning to cool with each day, it was still warm enough to sleep with windows wide open. On harvest day the tractors pulling gondolas bounced and rattled their way down our road and drive. The shouts from workers mixed with the rumbling of equipment have become the most remembered sound of my childhood. They arrived as the sun was rising and their noise woke me before I was ready, but I did not care. Harvest day, the excitement and stirrings around it, was climactic. After this and the bustling of summer, life slowed.

In the fall, grape leaves begin to turn brittle and a sense of total dehydration is seen in the trees and smelled in the dusty fields. But this sensation does not last but a few weeks. With the end of picking season comes rain which makes the Sierra visible once again. The smell is distinct as precipitation stirs the fine dust of the dry summer. It is the smell of the first day of school. It always rained on that first day, just as predictable as strong breezes on June evenings, blowing caps and gowns at commencement exercises. It is a mad rush for those farmers who have laid raisins. They will quickly mold if they get wet, so out comes the gondolas and trailers with family and friends who must save the brown-wrapped raisins from ruin. As the grapes are being picked, the oranges which climb up to base of the Sierra foothills are ripening. They will be packed, frost permitting, until the heat of an early summer sets in again.

Valley summers are unrelentingly hot. Country roads, lined by grapevines and fruit trees, waver. The emergence of trucks and their trailers hauling bins of nectarines, peaches, plums, and apricots only seem to intensify the swelter. Billowing exhaust and stirred up dust add to the haze, and grayness settles before the Sierra and its foothills which were visible only a month prior. But it is in the summer that this valley comes alive.

The first Spanish-Californian ranchers brought large herds of cattle into the region, yet what they carried in their pockets would lead to a larger, more lasting business for the San Joaquin Valley. These were peach pits which were planted on land grants along the rivers. Here, the fruit flourished beside grapes which once grew wild along the river bottoms. Although these indigenous grapes soon disappeared with the diversion of needed waters, the very thought that these varieties could grow in the valley caught the attention of early white settlers. "It is probable," wrote a surveyor in 1853,

> that grapes could be cultivated in this valley with success. The borders of the creek were overgrown in places by thick masses of grapevines, loaded with long and heavy clusters of fruit. This grape is deserving of attention, as it is probable that it will be found an exceedingly valuable variety for the manufacture of wine.

Although this native grape would vanish from the valley, many more wine and table varieties such as Muscat, Red Flame, and the most populous, the Thompson seedless, primarily used for raisins and wine "filler" due to it heavy sugar quantity, took its place in this region. These first vineyards also grew in the soil along the Kings River.

As farming spread across the landscape, the pattern of produce was reminiscent of the vegetation pattern of years before—citrus near the eastern foothills, tree fruit and grapes in the sandy loam soil where the river flows its strongest through the valley, and alfalfa and cotton in the alkali of the Tulare Lake Basin. It was predicted early on from propagandists such as Titus Cronise to writers such as Frank Norris, that this land would produce a great fortune. Norris writes in *The Octopus*,

> It was the season after the harvest, and the great earth, the mother, after its period of

production, its pains of labour, delivered of the
fruit of its loins, slept the sleep of exhaustion in
the infinite repose of the colossus, benignant,
eternal, strong, the nourisher of nations, the
feeder of an entire world.

As the success of growing fruit was realized, many varieties
from the east and abroad were brought in and tested. As
the landscape changed so would the varieties of fruit
which came and left the valley floor. Cronise described
the varieties of peaches, plums, apricots, and grapes which
were beginning to be planted in the valley as early as the
1860s. The Early York peach and Columbia plum suggest
their native eastern homes. These varieties changed by the
turn of the century to hybrids or other varieties which grew
better, shipped better, and sold for a higher price. These
same factors are still changing the varieties of fruit grown
in the valley today.

In his book *Epitaph for a Peach* local farmer and writer,
David Mas Masumoto, examines the fate of his Sun Crest
peach. The fruit is of superior quality concerning taste, but
its dull color does not attract the customer's eye, and its
juiciness does not sustain a long shelf life. "'Consumers
love the new varieties,'" a broker tells Masumoto. "'They'll
abandon your old Sun Crests.'" A third generation grower
of stone fruit, Masumoto goes on to express his love for
farming, which encompasses tradition and heritage. This
passion has led him to plant Elberta peaches, a vintage
variety only known to the old-timers. It, as with his Sun
Crest, does not ship well. His solution was to create an
"Adopt a Peach" program where, upon harvest day, all
adoptive participants arrive at his farm ready to pick their
own fruit from their own adopted tree. This hands-on

appreciation for the process—planting, feeding, protecting, and harvesting—makes one respect the work and lives involved. The undertaking is difficult and many aspects of it often taken for granted by those who have not labored within farming.

When one grows up in the rural San Joaquin Valley, it is a given that the summers of youth are spent working in a packing shed. One of the many lessons learned by such a job is that American consumers are picky. Sometimes more fruit goes down the cull line than the pack line with pieces which are too small, irregularly shaped, or otherwise undesirable. Fruit blemishes ever so slight are thrown out. A scattering of tiny red dots known as sunburn—out; the least bit soft—throw it; the smallest stem puncture or insect bite—the shopper won't buy it. But go to a place such as South America and the markets are full of soft, sutured, and over-ripened fruit that would have made its way down one of our cull lines. The fruit is still good, just not pretty.

It is common to see orchards ripped out of the ground after picking, leaving the soil upturned and bare. The variety, no longer receiving a good market price, is about to be replaced. Large piles of once blooming trees become an entangled mass of roots and leafless limbs. At night their burning sets an orange glow into the sky as the air begins to grow colder with the coming of fall. In the spring, new varieties are planted and the waiting begins until their first harvest, usually three years later. Not unlike corporate farming, the landscape is now determined by the desires of people who do not live on the land.

What has the ultimate voice, however, is nature herself. Farmers can influence the soil and plants with fertilizers and insecticides. They can girdle their grapes into lush and plump delicacies or choose to lay raisins instead of sending them to the winery. They pull waters from underground or from the irrigation ditches by the turning of a valve. But they cannot suppress the weather.

I was working in a fruit packing shed one early June day when an unseasonable storm controlled the valley. When the electricity went off, the roar of the skies could be heard. It was louder than the machinery that was spewing only a half-second before. We ran from the inside corridor of the shed to the front and stood on the loading dock. The storm had come.

The roar of hail was deafening on the metal roof. It was impossible to see through its screen which left us motionless and speechless for five minutes or more. Several inches piled up beside the building before it finally stopped. It was the storm of a lifetime; at least, by the end, the farmers and packers hoped it was.

In this region we are not used to such angry weather, especially in June when the fruit trees are abundant with ripening fruit that soon would be packed. The year's crops that had survived the usual scatterings of hail that we were used to, and the unseasonable sudden changes of hot to cold temperatures that we were not used to, were finished.

That evening at home I listened to local reports assessing the damage to area crops. Many plum, peach, and nectarine orchards were ruined. Grapes, still small and green, months away from picking, were also hurt. Even on the west side of the valley cotton fields did not survive. Almonds and other nuts in the northern end were stricken.

The shape of the hail was saucer-like, created that way by the strong horizontal wind currents above. When it blew through the orchards, hitting the fruit from the side, the hail acted as razor blades slicing the fruit with deep, open wounds. The fruit could be marketable if the damage stopped there. It could be packed at a lesser, utility grade which may bring at least a small profit for the grower. But the lesions leave way for brown rot which sometimes can go unnoticed on the grading tables but will, in a matter of days, grow and spread to other pieces in a packed box.

Two men on the local newscast squared off in debate. What was the cause for the devastating storm? The meteorologist had his theory. The reoccurring El Niño was responsible for California's uncommonly wet weather, its warm winter and cold spring which left much of the fruit up to then mushy. Next year would be back to normal.

The other man, an ecologist, had a much different idea. This was the price we were paying for years of abuse to the ozone layer and was not the result of a returning Pacific storm but the beginning of a permanent change in our valley, and world, climate.

At the time, I favored the El Niño theory. It coincided with the storm of over a dozen years before that left Tulare Lake full. Now, years later, the effects of global warming are more fully realized. I question what this means to what we now know as the landscape of the valley. It is no longer uncommon to have several weeks' worth of over 100 degree days in July and August, sometimes days at over 110. It has become a typical summer, not a heat wave. The snowfall amounts have continually dropped. Snow pack is melting earlier, and blooms come on the trees sooner in the spring.

As with so many visionaries who eagerly looked at the future of the valley's landscape, there are speculations. What will become of this valley whose very life is in its fields? What will this mean economically? What will this mean ecologically? What will be the valley's next pattern?

Some go so far as to contemplate whether the land could return to its natural state, reclaiming the landscape of over a century before. They see water once again seasonally gathering in vernal pools across the valley, and the Kings, which once fed millions of acres, regaining its grandeur, winding freely outside of man's intervention. They imagine Tulare Lake retrieving its shores, with its rebirth bringing back the hundreds of species which once called the lake home. And visualize previously plowed fields transforming themselves into the foliage of renewed native plants, a delta of California willows, endangered oaks, elderberry, and prairie of bull rush and salt grass able to flourish in soil along the river that had been overwhelmed by plows, pesticides, and fertilizers. Beavers, fish, and birds, predator and song, that used to live here only 150 years ago return home and replenish their numbers.

In reality, it took less than one hundred years to change this natural landscape into an agrarian oasis. It will take much longer than that, more than devastating storms and damaged ozone to retrieve a frontier. Farmers have grown used to challenges: years of devastating drought, the expanse of corporate farming, the spread of cities into the precious fields. As long as their love for their land remains, they will survive nature's wrath too.

14

Some are born in their place, some find it, some realize after long searching that the place they left is the one they have been searching for. But whatever their relation to it, it is made a place only by slow accrual, like a coral reef.

—Wallace Stegner,
A Sense of Place

MY FATHER WAS the only one of six living siblings who came back to the land of his parents and grandparents. Nostalgia may have, in part, spurred him. During the summers, from 1936-1939, my father, his parents, older brother and sister, drove ten hours through the valley and into Mariposa. They stayed with my grandfather's parents who had settled first on Sherlock Creek in 1857, then three miles down the road on Mariposa Creek. French Camp set down in a long, narrow valley with the creek winding through. The simple and unpainted wood-framed house was too small for all to sleep in. My father, the youngest, slept between his brother and sister in a small brass bed under the stars. Living in Los Angeles, they could not have imagined such a wondrous night sky. They sat out every night before bed listening to Virginia reels and to what would become most significant in my father's life, his parents' cheerful reminiscence of growing up on their valley homesteads.

In the mornings they helped with the vegetable farm, irrigating and picking string beans, carrots, and corn, my grandfather taking their harvest into Mariposa to sell. In the afternoons they worked the sluice box on the creek, shoveling dirt and directing water, collecting gold dust and a few small nuggets that their Uncle Bud would pan once he returned from work. The Apperson Mine, 10 miles from Mariposa, in Jerseydale, was profitless, so Uncle Bud worked for the Diltz and Spread Eagle Mines. His was the only legitimate income for the family since my grandfather didn't work and my great-grandfather, in his eighties, was on monthly provisions from the Hearst Corporation, even though his cousin Phoebe had been dead for nearly twenty years. A letter from one of William Randolph Hearst's attorneys mentions an interview ironically conducted on Labor Day and outlines the agreement:

> Sept. 24, 1936
> Mr. J. K. Apperson
> Sherlock's Creek,
> California.

> Dear Mr. Apperson:
> Doubtless you will recall my visit with you and Mrs. Apperson on Labor Day. I made a report of it, setting forth your relationship to Mr. Hearst as you outlined it to me, and sent the report to one of Mr. Hearst's executives. He advises that Mr. Hearst has instructed that the

enclosed check be sent you and that a check for a similar amount be sent you monthly until we are advised to the contrary. There are no restrictions upon the use of the money. It is Mr. Hearst's hope that you will get some benefit and enjoyment from it.

I trust you and Mrs. Apperson are enjoying good health.

The checks to the family ended when great-grandpa died three years later. Once again, other means would have to be found.

Los Angeles, at the time, was a fine place to live. Although there were increasing jobs to be had from the Depression to the war years, my father's family was very poor, mainly because my grandfather was occupied with thoughts of gold. One photo of my grandfather has him standing shovel in hand beside his father on Mariposa Creek in French Camp. A six-foot-long sluice box is set in the stream, and a heavy layer of snow, a rarity for this region, covers the ground in the ravine and on the trees behind and mountains above them. He has written on the back of the photo, "Kimble and I working a sluice box in the creek—it did not pan out." Perhaps the worst day of mining was better than the best day of traditional work.

From a young age, Dad and his brothers and sister sold newspapers on street corners to help subsidize their relief money. They roomed in Aunt Lorraine's boarding house and played amid asphalt and concrete of their industrial neighborhood, near downtown. In the hills, their poverty was not as apparent; they could live off the land, wear dusty overalls, and forgo shined shoes for Mass. His favorite memories were of the open spaces of his summers. In one photo Dad, along with his brother and sister, march single file along the road above French Camp, pith helmets on their heads and their own small pick axes and shovels carried on their shoulders.

I recognize this road. When I was eight years old, I took a trip there with my father. There is a photograph of us standing in front of a dilapidated gate and sagging barbed-wire fence. I have long pigtails and my father and I look as if we dressed alike, both wearing white shirts and socks and blue shorts. There is an oak tree a few feet behind the gate, and we stand in its shadow. Even if I didn't have this photograph to trigger some of the details, I still would have remembered this day. I recall the dusty road above having deep grooves and "washboard" from that spring's rains and its steep descent into the small valley below. The grasses had grown tall and were already browned in the early summer heat. That oak tree was a comfort after what seemed a very long walk for an eight-year-old. There were no structures left standing, but there was an abandoned bed frame, an artifact that jogged a memory for my father, explaining how he, his brother and sister, slept. Those were four idyllic summers for him. We were there because Dad had heard the property was for sale, and he was interested in buying it, acquiring as closely as possible his favorite memories of childhood. "For old-time's sake," he once said. He wanted to camp-out, spend his weekends in the solace of wonted surroundings.

After he had a family of his own, he and my mom decided to leave the city and move to land they could call their own. When I asked my father once why he moved us to the San Joaquin Valley, he simply said, "This is home to me."

"This was your parents' home," I pushed one day when the timing seemed to be right.

He set his jaw and examined the backs of his rough hands, as he often does when he is deep in thought. "This place has always seemed to me our *family's* home. It is just where we belong."

The farmer is, perhaps, a romantic ideal. My grandfather, the perpetual dreamer, was happy in the hills raising his apple crop and mining for a few nuggets. The back-breaking aspect of farmer diminishes when one thinks of working your hands into dirt you call your own. The creation involved in making something grow, of nourishing and harvesting, calls to our sensitivities. In the best of situations it possibly becomes a life you choose instead of one that is chosen for you. California, the San Joaquin Valley in particular, was an empty slate, a place where lives could begin again, more prosperous than what was had before.

THE ATTRACTION TO this place was difficult for me to grasp when I was younger, but it has slowly come to make sense as I make the choice to keep the valley my home. There is a pull, a familial draw to this landscape. From my great-grandparents who, no matter their endeavors in the Sierra Nevada goldmines, kept their valley land as the foundation, to my father who returned his family to the land, there is a comfort. Perhaps it is the reassurance of the familiar or the contentment of belonging to a community that keeps us in one place.

In one of the many handkerchief and stationery boxes my grandmother kept filled with brittle sympathy cards, mining claims, and Western Union Telegrams, there is a carefully folded stack of newspaper clippings from the *Hanford Daily Sentinel* of the 1930s. The "Social Doings" section contains the monthly meetings of the Kings County Club at Los Angeles. My grandmother and her sisters were members of this club of two dozen women, old school friends and neighbors among them, whose roots were in the Hanford and Lemoore area. Detailed accounts of birthday luncheons and house-warmings are chronicled in classic 1930s "society page" prose. One clipping mentions:

> The high light of the afternoon was a picture exhibit, photographs taken long ago of the girls of the club, many of whom are white-haired grandmothers. There was much laughter over the pictures of bald-headed babies, comical maids in pigtails, important young ladies in their teens and charming young women of the gay nineties. Then, too, there were pictures of family groups that made smiling eyes misty, pictures of loved faces that are only a beautiful memory now.

Also among the boxes is an autograph book that belonged to my great aunt Lorraine during the 1890s. Neighbors, friends, and cousins left school-day remembrances, lofty truisms, and simply, yet beautifully executed signatures. "My dearest Lulu," is how most of them begin with the date and town, mostly stating Lemoore, as a part of their salutation. Even on Grandmother's prayer cards handed out at her funeral in 1979, it is stated, "Genevieve Apperson, Native of Lemoore, California." In nearly every document, it seems, the people and the place are distinctly interlinked.

History of place and the power it has in our lives is not taught in school, and perhaps only barely mentioned to our children when we speed by an historical marker or flip the pages of a family album. So we do not question our parents, or grandparents if we are so established to a locale, about the decisions that were made, the factors or sacrifices. Still others don't question why they stay once they are able to leave. I have been blessed to be raised with stories, stories of strife and the vitality that emerged, stories of joy within the journey. I keep thinking about my great-great-grandmother, Margaret Watts Hays, and how she had to wait 25 trying years before her desire of coming to California was fulfilled; I envision my great-grandmother, Katherine O'Connor Beaver, the age of my daughter, being physically shaken as their ship rounded Cape Horn. I close my eyes, and with the help of photographs, documents, and letters in their own hands, can almost put myself among my ancestors to relive in my mind their adventures and try to understand their perceptions of their place in the landscape they came to.

MY MOTHER HAS been the one constant for keeping these stories alive, no matter which side of the family she offered to us. When I was very young, my brother and sister in school, my mother took me in her wood-paneled, blue station wagon exploring country roads and neighboring counties. This was my schooling. Mom needed to get herself grounded in her new surroundings. We stopped at antique stores, and while mom rifled through trays of silverware and inspected the needlepoint of well-used linens my job was to look through the stacks of sepia photos for resemblances to my father's family, for images lost among the years, given up by family members who did not prize them. Mom was the one who never asked, "Why would you want to know that?" when I pressed for the obscure or private. All events were important to the larger narrative of family and sense of home and place. She described all she knew.

Though Dad's family were among the early pioneers in the state, Mom's family came west with a better known story. Like so many thousands, they trekked from Oklahoma during the Great Depression. Though better off than Steinbeck's Joad family, they too left at a time of economic upheaval and emotional despair. There simply was no future for my grandfather, Fred Peck, in the tri-state area of Oklahoma, Missouri and Kansas other than work in the lead mines. His father-in-law was a foreman for one of the largest mines in the area which employed many of the men in both families.

My mother was born two days after the Crash. For the next month, while my grandmother, Estelle, was taking care of her new baby, my grandfather nursed my grandmother's father as he lay dying of TB, a condition so common to those working in the mines. In the early spring of 1930, my great-grandfather dead just a few months along with most of the members of my grandmother's family, my grandfather decided it was their time to leave, going westward to everything that California promised. They packed all they could take in their Model T and left Miami, Oklahoma. They never regretted their decision.

Unlike the 110,000 "Okies" that settled in the San Joaquin Valley as tenant sharecroppers, they went to Los Angeles where better jobs awaited, especially if someone had a trade. My grandfather, an established carpenter and dabbling inventor, always had employment. The war years brought even more work and opportunity. He helped build the Los Angeles Coliseum and worked on Howard Hughes' Spruce Goose while my grandmother became a WAC. While my uncle went to war, my mother traveled stateside as a dancer in the USO and opened her own dance studio in Hollywood. California had provided.

Throughout the earlier years, the family grew restless and left Los Angeles, moving around the southwest to New Mexico, Texas, and Arizona, but each time they returned to California. Moving so often, "home" was not something my mom felt as a child, but it was an ideal she wanted to have one day for her own family. Home did not mean the same thing to her parents. Not once did my grandparents revisit the places of their youth on the Neosho River, among what an idle viewer would see as much plusher surroundings. Going back was not something that was done. People of the past generations always seemed to look forward.

My parents looked forward by looking to simpler ways. They wanted to leave the populous congestion, schedules which prevented Dad from spending time with his children on weekdays, and weekends when children chose to not play outside because the smog hurt their lungs. At age forty, my parents, two pre-teenagers and I, a toddler, picked up and left for the valley, a slower paced life and a connection to a place my parents thought was missing in their lives. My father felt farming was in his blood.

Although I was, for years, unhappy with my parents' choice to move to the valley, I always admired their making the decision to begin anew. To pick up what roots they had created in the suburbs of Los Angeles, leave friends and family, and promise their children that a more simple life was a better life, takes courage. I am reminded of the generations of ancestors which lead to this moment and the expansive moves across oceans and states. This, too, becomes a romantic ideal, liberating at the very least. I always thought I would do the same some day, but as I approach my parents' age when they moved, I feel more grounded, intent now, in keeping this place my home. I had pictured myself moving to northern California where the beaches and mountains seem tranquil, the small-scale farming more pastoral and cautious. Although nowhere in California can escape the urban sprawl, there seem to be many regions to the north where taking a step into nature is without trespass, less of a distance and more abundant.

Instead, I moved to a house that was built during the housing boom of the 1990s. For ten years my mother drove me to school passing where my home is now. It was plum orchards then. I distinctly remember the light of the afternoons shining through the rows of trees creating a strobe light-like effect as we passed, and if being irrigated on one of those hot afternoons, the temperature would drop as soon as we entered the orchard's elongating shadows. Again, the conflict arises. Not able to afford a farm, I settled for a new house on the edge of a development where we can look out our kitchen window and watch the sun rise over the Sierra, see the canal, a few crops of grapes, blueberries, and kiwi, and if we strain our necks far enough to the north, my parents' home.

Perhaps it is knowing that it is human nature to want what you have not experienced, believing that the grass is, especially in this case, always greener somewhere else that has been one more factor in keeping me here, settled me in to a suburban setting I thought I would come to escape. It is family and friends, of course, that draws me, but also a personality that fights for the underdog and a tenacious curiosity to see what will become of the farmland and preserves, rivers and lakebed, during my lifetime.

Outside my kitchen window, I saw the ditch-tenders slowly drive their tanker truck spraying what few weeds continued to live on into yet another unseasonably hot spring. On the opposite bank next to the blueberry grove a young oak tree is unaffected by the 100 degree heat and out of reach, at least for now, from the ditch-tender. I will check its progress daily, smile at its steadfastness against certain demise as I witness the cycle of renewal I am reminded of at this time of year. Perhaps someday a mighty oak will grow there undisturbed, giving sanctuary to a red tail hawk, a burrowing owl at its base. My smile broadens, content with my home.

15

Therein lies the element of permanence for those who have possessed the land, have tilled it and passed it on undamaged to another generation in an unbroken family heritage.

—Brooks D. Gist,
The Years Between

AS A CHILD I played in the turned up dirt among housing construction stakes and newly poured sidewalks near a friend's house on the other side of town. In a fit of orneriness, I would pull up stakes and throw them like javelins into the stagnant summer air. That long ago I knew what was coming. I overheard my parents talk about our farm and the coming threat of subdivisions. How could they afford to keep the farm if they were annexed into the city? And I also knew that all of the farmers that shielded my parents from the town were aging. Their children had moved to the city as soon as they graduated from high school. Others didn't have children to leave their places to. I could see the way it would become, and I was right. As the aged died, their children received a good inheritance after selling the land to developers. Most of the houses weren't worth much, after the owner lost a spouse and wasn't able to keep up the place. Other farmers, after a lifetime of backbreaking work, retired into an easier life as they sold the land around their own dwelling, leveling the richest farming region twenty acres at a time. This is what happened to the land where I live now. To the small towns of the valley, growth means prosperity. The enticing propaganda sent to the east over a century ago is seen today in billboards along Highway 99 as land developers, as they are called, advertise the valley's newest face. According to the Department of Conservation, nearly twenty thousand acres of farm and graze land in Fresno, Kings, Merced, Madera, and Tulare counties were lost to non-agricultural uses in a recent three-year span, an average of nearly twenty-six acres a day. It has been predicted that Fresno County alone will lose an estimated 20% of its agricultural land over the next forty years as the population in this region is expected to triple. What is lost is not only farmland but close-knit communities which once formed because its people had a deep connection and respect for the land which was their livelihood. What is difficult to understand is that there is so much greed and no one talks of misgivings. The price of land is tempting, so I suppose not many would turn down such a deal. My father, though, has had regrets.

Where the old Beaver ranch house once stood is a narrow section of vacant land scattered with tumbleweeds and clover. It rests here, momentarily, between a subdivision and six rows of abandoned, brittle grapevines. At the end of these rows is a gnarled pile of grape stumps, wire, stakes, and drip irrigation line. Next to the last row, a determined palm tree, only eight feet tall, grows from its parent stump and matches those seen in photos of my great-grandparents' farm. Within one small view, what was my family's ranch, is spoiled yet presently undisturbed land, cultivated field, and housing tract all in one. It is the three faces of the San Joaquin Valley. A sale sign just beyond this pile advertises a commercial sale; no doubt this land will become a strip mall or industrial park.

Several years ago Dad and I stopped at the southern end of the family ranch on the day we tried to find the remains of Tulare Lake. This section of the property had just been razed. Orange tape and surveying equipment cluttered the short-lived bare lot, a sign with red flags waving advertised the housing tract's name. Ironically, subdivisions are named in respect of the very thing they deface: Pheasant Grove, Meadow Estates, Plum Orchard, Peach Vista. Dad leaned against the pick-up truck, arms crossed, and looked out across the land. He told me about the court battle with his cousins which occurred when his mother asked him to sell the property in the late 1960s. The cousins wanted to keep it. They could envision the money it would bring in one day as developments moved closer. I know Dad was torn. The money from the land was needed for the continuing care of his aunt, my grandmother's mentally ill older sister, Myrtle, whom she took care of all her life. But Dad valued the land and the lives that worked it. Now all that is left of my grandmother's family as a sign that they were a part of this area are the graves of her parents and grandparents and a quilt in a museum. Gone are their farmhouse and barn, the irrigation pump and scatterings of plows, and the trees and lawns planted as a symbol of their resilience.

The first houses built in the San Joaquin Valley were much like my great grandparents'. They were square, wooden homesteads, many with screened in porches which crossed the entire front of the house. They lacked any ornamentation, were usually white, and as barren in appearance as the virgin land on which they stood. If there was a lack of decorative landscaping it was, in most cases, a good indication of the dwellers' attitude toward the land. Their attachment to the place was not strong. There would be no need to embellish the residence if there was a good chance they would be moving on to more promising surroundings. Practicality was the main concern. On the other hand, if a home was more than the average square, wood-plank house and gave in to the least amount of architectural fads or had any amount of ornamental landscaping, it was assumed the family would stay, making the valley their home.

As small fortunes grew, the farmhouse became more elaborate following the style of the Victorian era. Gingerbread and gambrel roofs became common for those who could afford them. The wrap-around porch replaced the screened-in porch which was moved for aesthetic reasons to the back of the house. Unpainted clapboard siding would no longer suffice. Homes were painted the bright yellows and blues of the Victorian period. Along with decorative trees and flower beds, lawns and gardens filled the space around the home which was not planted in crops. By the turn of the century, the valley was teeming with not only beautiful dwellings, but new and exotic plants previously unknown to the valley landscape. Canary Island date and California fan palm trees lined long dirt roads leading to homes surrounded by verdant orchards. Shrubbery were planted and trimmed to shape, and a palette of geraniums and mums colored flower beds which had no real practicality. These decorations were there only for sheer refinement in what had been a harsh wilderness only decades before.

One photo of the Beaver ranch shows two of my grandmother's sisters sitting on the top step of the front porch. The front yard is being flood irrigated, the same way my parents water their front yard to this day. There are two symmetrically planted palm trees on either side of the front walkway. The edge of the yard is outlined with a row of what looks like pansies or primrose, their petals just above the water line.

I WAS ABLE to find the locations of my family's farms in this region using the *1892 Thompson Historical Atlas Map of Tulare County*. At the time, Tulare County also comprised what was to become Kings County in 1893. In it is descriptions of the commerce and agriculture of each town within the county. The more wealthy landowners, once being enticed by the book's publisher to boast their wealth and position in the community, commissioned the publisher's artists to draw representations of their farms to be printed in the book. In each of these idealized lithographs, presented from a bird's-eye view, is a stately Victorian farmhouse and outbuildings, some with corrals, wagons and horses. There is a sense of sterility and order in their perfectly straight lines. Fences, barns, homes, and even horse teams are rigidly aligned to streets and railroads. Fruit trees, shown in perfectly proportioned rows, are identical to one another. It was just what the landowners wanted to share with family and friends they had left behind in the east. They had brought order to an inhospitable land and in returned were rewarded by great wealth.

When I look at these drawings I am reminded of a photograph of my parents' farm that was taken when I was a child. A photographer came to our door selling a scene he would take on the first good-weather day from his airplane. My parents bought, and a few months later received the 16X20 color print which they promptly framed and has been on display in their dining room ever since. It is a pleasant photo taken from the southeast catching a slight view of the front of the house and most of the vineyard that surrounded. The photographer fit in the canal, full with water, in the bottom left of the picture and both barns. It is an archival piece now since one of the barns and the massive mulberry tree in the backyard are gone, the traditionally white house has been given color, there is a swimming pool where the garden was, and the vineyard has been replaced with stone fruit. Unlike the drawings of a century before, the photo has character. It must have been taken on a day in the early spring as there is a mixture of green and brown grasses growing on the canal bank and the Japanese magnolia and mulberry tree are budded, but not full enough with leaves to cover the house, and the vineyards have enough foliage to know that it is thriving. I see it now as pastoral.

I remember my mother telling the story of one of our neighbors, also commissioning the same photographer to take an aerial photo. The husband called and found out what day the photographer would be buzzing his farm. Early in the morning on that day, after seeing his wife off to the hairdresser, he pulled out every farming implement that he owned from the barn. There were several tractors, discers, a scraper, fork lifts, and gondolas. He lined them up beside the barn and down the dirt avenue leading to the back of his property. He, like those early settlers in the valley who commissioned their own artists to portray their homes, wanted to show his prosperity. He was proud of what he had obtained. Those implements made it possible.

Another farmer, C. F. Winell, was a "progressive citizen" according to a headline in our town's newspaper in 1910. He came to the area just prior to the turn of the century. Near penniless, he found a farm to rent and hired himself out to other farmers when his crop would allow. He was ill prepared when the first harvest came; he had no trays on which to lay his raisins. While out looking for a friendly farmer whose trays he might borrow, he spied another crop which was for sale. He bought it later that day after persuading the local banker that the crop would pay for itself and then some. It did, and Winell became one of the major landowners in the area, buying yet more land along the way.

In 1905, Winell built the home I grew up in. A copy of his story, along with photos of both the house and Winell and his wife, hang along the staircase of our house among our own family photos. They have become family just as the home has.

The earliest picture of the site is consistent with the early settlements. A small square framed house sits upon dusty ground which is plowed right up to the front stoop. The wood is unpainted, including the screen door in the shadows of the small covered porch situated on the right side of the house. The only ornamentation is a four foot palm tree which grows beside the porch. In the distance are rows of grapevines and closer to the house a few fruit trees. In front of these, on either side of the dwelling, are three men. Two stand beside a white horse pulling a wagon, and one man stands on a buckboard, reins in hand which lead to a brown horse with a slumping back. One of these men, dressed in overalls and wearing a wide-brimmed hat which shades his eyes, is Winell.

The rest of the photographs show close to what the house looks like today. The original dwelling on the site was either torn down or possibly became the foundation for the larger, more domesticated home. In two of these photos, one taken from the west and another from the east, Winell stands near the two story house as his wife sits gracefully on the lawn beside him. Shrubs and more palm trees surround the house which is painted the more typical farmhouse-white (supposedly to reflect the summer's heat) with black screens on the windows. The siding consists of both clapboard and decorative fishtail shingles with bric-a-brac shaped in a bow at the front and back eves of the house reaching to the point of the gambrel roof. As with the porch of the original house, it is built to the right of the front of the house where a railing and turned posts curve around to enclose the space. Two chimneys reach up from the unusually steep roof, one going to the kitchen and the other to the octagon-shaped living room. This fireplace was oddly boarded up until my parents unearthed it. It was a small opening meant for a coal burner, but it had never been used. Typical for the homes in the valley, the back porch is a screened-in room which has since been altered to solid walls and windows. In all, few alterations have been made to the structure of the home. Winell had installed plumbing, constructing the first indoor bathroom in the area. At the time it was seen as a vulgar fixture to have in the home. Passersby used to call Winell equally crude names and continue the assault by throwing dirt clods at the house. Perhaps this is why he also built an outhouse which still stands behind the barn.

Behind the house is the tank house, or pump house as they are sometimes called. This is a three-story tower at times attached to a single-story storeroom. The water tank is housed on the third story. Water was pumped straight up from the ground into the tank and then gravity fed into the house. Although tank houses still exist across the valley, many people do not know their purpose.

All in all, the house and buildings such as the barn, which stores the farm's original hand plows along with one of my great-grandfather's, the tank house and outhouse all look as they did. The house's original woodwork and stained-glass windows are preserved along with most of the electrical fixtures which were added in the early twenties. My parents bought the house with a glance and a nod to each other within moments of seeing it. They worked for years preserving it and making it a home for us. My sister and brother remember several houses they lived in Los Angeles before I was born, but this is the only home I had ever known, and although I am married now, this house and the land on which it sits will always be home to me. I cannot picture my parents anywhere but here. My mom belongs in her garden, every spring renewing that sign of over a century ago where ornamentation suggests contentment, and my father belongs walking the orchard.

In my photo album I have a photograph of Dad as he completed planting the last row of new vines. He stands dust-covered with both gloves in one hand and wears a brimmed hat reminiscent of Winell's. It is very different from his suits and ties of the city. Most of my grandmother's pictures of growing up in the valley are taken in the fields. Her older sisters would picnic amid the furrows of alfalfa. In one, two of these sisters are eating lunch. They sit on a blanket that spreads across a shallow ditch between two furrows. Even though they wear large hats to block the sun, they still squint at the camera. The following is accurately concluded and written on the back of this photo: "One good ditch and plenty of water worth a hundred poor ones and no water." There is something impassioned about being out on the land you work and knowing that land, getting its dirt under your fingernails and brushing its dust from your clothes.

Ours is a small farm, one mile west of the Kings River. Twenty acres of Thompson seedless, wine grapes, has recently been replanted with popular white flesh and sub-acid nectarines, their brilliant magenta blossoms in the spring and fall foliage giving the farm a more broad palette. Two English walnut trees mark each corner at the back of the property. It is common to see a red-tailed hawk in one of these trees, keeping an eye out for mice which scurry through the fields. At least once a year we see a crane along the canal bank or, more frequently, spy a coyote's skittish trot through the neighboring vines, stopping now and again, looking around to see where he's been. In the early morning, groups of pheasant and quail cross the yard searching for food, especially in the days after flood-irrigating the front lawn. And in the evenings, the echo of an owl, which has made the barn his home, makes the night peaceful.

I have within me memories of conflicting themes. As a child, the darkness and stillness around the farm at night actually frightened me. I fed the peacocks as they came to roost. The walk to the barn, flashlight in hand, was quick-paced. The return to the house became a run as I headed for the light of the back porch. In the winter, the wind blew the English walnut tree outside my bedroom window, scratching at the glass and shallow balcony. As the wind blew harder, the stairs creaked, making falling asleep a struggle. I imagined the second owner of our house, who had died there and whose funeral service was held on our front porch, climbing the stairs, turning at the landing, and ascending to my bedroom door where the stairs ended.

However, this was winter. There was comfort in the noises of summer where bullfrogs in the canal reminded me that I wasn't alone since it was easy to believe no one else existed on such normally still nights, only a slight breeze coming through open windows near my bed. In recollect, in summer my appreciation for where I lived seemed to grow as I could play like friends who lived in neighborhoods could not. While friends in town were a walk away from the community pool, there was more enjoyment to be had in the four inches of water that gushed across our flooded lawn. On the days the water did not come from the well in the vineyard, the water was pumped from the canal. I collected empty mayonnaise jars filled with tadpoles which I kept until they sprouted back legs, and then released them back into the canal. The usually sharp needles from the deodar cedars that hurt to walk on became a soft floating bed of mulch. The irrigation of the vineyard was almost as enjoyable. Icy water gurgling from each row's pipe cut the sandy soil creating rich brown furrows of moisture, the light dirt of the berm looking as if it all could blow away from what lay below. Once wet, this powdery soil made the best mud pies while legs sunk calf-deep into the dirt.

We replanted the back 33 rows of vines when I was seven. I don't remember much about being seven, who my friends were at the time, or the daily presence of my brother and sister at home, but I do remember us taking out and replanting that vineyard. Following behind the vintage 1949 Ford tractor and wagon I threw on top what stumps, crossarms, and stakes I could carry and then, going back through, dropped off each new vine to be planted. It was early October, so with the forgotten Muscat grapes still holding fast to the vine, my brother, sister, and I had a rotten grape fight. I pegged my brother in the back of the neck as he drove the tractor, leaving sticky juice running down his back, staining his shirt, gnats collecting around his collar. It was a great victory for a little sister. I learned to drive that tractor a few years later. Still a lightweight, I had to raise myself from the seat and throw one leg over it placing both feet on the clutch to shift gears. Stopping, too, required all my weight plus jumping up and down pumping the brake, just missing the barn each time.

This is where I came when I broke up with my first boyfriend. This is where we walked, arms around my father, when Grandma died. Any time I feel disconnected, this is where I go. Any time I need to withdraw, I take a walk in familiar surroundings. Like my father, I find comfort in the connection and familiarity of the land. The farm and its fate are on my mind continuously as I realize how close *this* landscape could be to the brink of extinction.

16

You could cover the whole world with asphalt, but sooner or later green grass would break through.
—Ilya Ehrenburg, attributed

THE CONCERNS OVER urban sprawl, coupled with high estate taxes, have spurred a surge of farmland preservation groups both federal and private. The California Farmland Conservancy Program, California Department of Conservation, Great Valley Center, Growth Alternative Alliance, American Farmland Trust, and the list goes on and on, are all working to keep what is commonly called the "working landscape" intact and safe from being paved-over. The Williamson Act began in 1965. It alone is responsible for preserving more than sixteen million acres of farmland in California by offering tax benefits. My parents, fearful of heavy city taxes on their acreage if they were annexed, saw placing their farmland into the Act a smart choice.

Preservation of both farmland and natural spaces may seem a paradox. When one thinks of natural spaces, farming is not the first image envisioned. Farming, as we have learned in this region, has been the predicament that replaced the native flora and fauna. Still, there is great pride in the enterprise and awe in the outcome, from the idealized notion of what it is to be a farmer to the necessity and grand scale of the product. Once again, the valley is comprised of contradictory elements.

If some are right who believe that nature's destruction comes from human's innate desire to control it, could it also be true that once it is nearly gone, we instinctively begin to nurture it?

From the time plows first cut into the valley soil, farmers have gone to any steps possible to ensure high crop yield. At the edges of crops which have recently been sprayed with pesticides or sulfur are signs with skull and crossbones, warnings to stay clear of the fields. The same approach is used along roadsides and canal banks as tanker trucks slowly spray herbicides. Game birds are left without refuge. Aesthetics are lost.

The Central Valley is distinguished as having, in its original state, one of the most distinctive and diverse grasslands in North America, with plants such as iodine brush and alkali heather being the only plants able to thrive in the naturally alkali earth. In the Tulare Basin region specifically, only eight percent of the scrub and salt brush habitat remain. Only four percent of the original wetlands survive with less than one percent of the developed water supply reaching them. One percent of original riparian woodland and less than one percent of the valley oak woodland has lasted.

Due to responses related largely to endangered species concerns, preservation of prairie and riparian habitats by both government and private conservancies has increased. The tule elk, San Joaquin kit fox, yellow-billed cuckoo, and California tiger salamander, to name just a wide-ranging few now have homes in safe havens of the Tule Elk Refuge, Kaweah Oaks Preserve, Kern National Wildlife Refuge, and Nature Conservancy's Pixley Reserve. Native riparian forests are given the opportunity to flourish. Natural wetlands are being restored to their original support for wildlife. The Tulare Basin Wildlife Partners, which is sustained by more than 70 collaborative groups and individuals, work to balance use and nature through a number of land and water conservation projects, including the 8,000 acre Ton Tache Lake restoration project located at what was Tulare Lake's Atwell Island. Here, native plants are reintroduced on reclaimed wetlands. Water channels are designed to mimic natural slough patterns. Evaporation ponds along Sand Ridge welcome birds as farmers return their least productive land to these efforts through a land retirement program. A healthy balance of farmland and wildlife is determined as rare plant and animal species are provided safe haven in a medley of vernal pools, riparian forest, and oak woodlands covering over a present 600,000 acres.

The Kern Wildlife Refuge, for another, serves as a stop for thousands of birds migrating along the Pacific Flyway. In the best of winters, upwards of 80,000 waterfowl settle-in. Swamp timothys, hard-stemmed bulrushes, and burhead grow among the riparian forest of Goodings willow and Fremont cottonwood trees while burrowing owls and snowy egrets feed on displaced frogs and insects as the irrigated swamp land is filled. This reliable supply of water is due to the 1992 Central Valley Project Improvement Act. A cornerstone for all these efforts is educating the public, providing us with a fuller understanding of the circumstance we have inherited and a glimpse of the landscape from which it grew.

With the trend toward organic and specialty farming and an awareness of imperiled animals, it seems that attitudes are changing with farmers as well. No longer is it the few altruistic farmers who chose not to blast the Valley oak from their symmetrical fields being conscientious. The organic industry has boomed, making organic farming viable for growers to practice. Also emerging is the specialty crop business. New varieties of blueberries that can survive the summer's heat are being harvested. These farmers, along with tree fruit to melon growers have found a new niche and are working directly with consumers at farmers' markets, local supermarkets and buyers, many of them restaurants in the metropolitan areas to the north and south. More farmers are now experimenting with cover crops of red clover, barley, or vetch, depending on the crop and time of year, which not only enrich the soil but act as a natural pesticide, reducing the amount of chemicals used. Solarization, where the moist soil of row crops is covered with plastic during several weeks in the summer, kills diseases, insects, and weed seeds, forgoing herbicides and pesticides.

Farmers in the northern region of the San Joaquin Valley have been much more active with their restoration efforts. There they are encouraged to build water ponds which fill in the summers with irrigation run-off. This salvages valuable water and, at the same time, becomes a haven for waterfowl. Windbreaks and hedgerows situated in corridors around crop rows also create home to animal life. The farm becomes a restored landscape which is once again able to support native species including a variety of helpful insects which aid in controlling the harmful ones. With the introduction of such an ecosystem, the farm's maintenance is actually reduced. Away from individual farms, native grasses are planted along roads and canal banks. Roadsides are being transplanted with native perennials. These grasses are naturally drought tolerant and fire resistant, and because they have such superior root systems they push out the introduced weeds. Erosion control occurs not only along these roadsides, but on canal banks which are not unlike the one across from my parents' farm. Besides controlling erosion, the plants shelter the surface of the water, slowing the evaporation in the sweltering summer months, possibly replacing a recent trend to put canals underground. Barren banks become, like the farms they feed, habitat for wildlife. The perennial grasses are a sanctuary for nesting as well as being an ecosystem of nutrients which have been depleted. One can only hope that it will be a short matter of time before some of these practices are seen in this region of the valley as well. Although a few pockets of Valley oak are seen planted along the roadways in the Tulare Basin by the state's transportation office, they are stunted and pale, not able to grow well in the lakebed's alkali soil. Education is needed at all levels.

What continues to be worrisome is the scarcity of local history being taught in our schools that includes a lack of information about Native American settlements, geology, and plant and animal life once natural to this region. Ask any number of adults to name a native plant, what chemical is being sprayed in the orchard next door, or about Tulare Lake and too often the response is silence. The real tragedy is when the silence becomes a shrug of indifference.

17

I look out on the upper
*   branches*
of a knowing old tree
*   and realize that I could step*
*   out this window*
and walk on top of the
*   universe*
but I prefer flat farmland
*   and the dry and tedious*
*   for my brief stay*
                        —Wilma Elizabeth McDaniel,
                                Self-Knowledge

AS A CHILD and teenager, I despised living in the valley. I treasured our house. It was historic and beautiful, but its surroundings depressed me. The towns were small, the weather was pleasant for much too brief of a period, and the landscape, frankly, bored me. There was little retreat from miles upon miles of cropland. Our isolated farm, although relatively close to town, felt miles from where "real" lives were being lived. It was lonesome for me, especially once my sister and brother left home. Days were too quiet and there was an anxious need to fill time once homework and chores were finished. I read, created imaginary friends, and wrote stories of children my age in different surroundings: a girl with seven siblings, a boy in the city riding in buses and subways surrounded by noise and adventure, someone who discovered she could fly and leave her home without her parents noticing. When I used to travel through Los Angeles I would point through the smoggy haze to a cluster of a town situated between two freeways and say "that is where I am from." I was referring to a house I did not recall in a city of cities that I barely knew. Still, I felt this was my missing home, the place where I would find myself if I only had the chance. I listened to stories of the neighborhood my brother and sister grew up in in the San Fernando Valley in the 1960s. There were about 20 kids all around the same age, always enough to play baseball or ride bikes in packs through extensive housing developments. I, however, never had sidewalks to learn how to roller skate or skateboard. Bicycle riding was limited to our driveway because our one lane country road was "too dangerous." This resentment lasted through my narrow focus of teenage years. A Saturday night movie or shopping in a mall was a thirty-mile trek. The main concern became how to get out, out of the stifling small town and away from what I saw as a lifeless farm. The land, the region, meant little to me. I limited my view by believing that the place where I would find my happiness and sense of belonging was beyond the San Joaquin Valley, away from the farm where I was raised. After my sister and brother had left home I knew I wanted to follow suit. Thinking of it now, our words of discontent must have hurt our parents. They brought us here, to this place that my mother quickly grew to love and my father had a deep attachment. They only wanted a better life for their family, a place to create a home.

My father appreciated what I, at that time, could not. "If California were its own country we would be ranked seventh in the world in GNP . . . the richest state in the nation," he repeated to us regularly. As a teenager my head nodded in complacent agreement, still complaining, "But there is nothing to do here . . . it is so boring . . . if we still lived in Los Angeles there would be something to do."

AS A YOUNG and restless adult, I went back to my family's earliest roots, southern England and Wales. I was in the land that William Apperson had left nearly 350 years before. I found peacefulness in the ever-green hills and roads that curved upon each other, connecting hamlet to village. There was even quaintness in the industrial districts and cities. It was so contrary to my valley. And it became, in a short matter of time, all too much of charm with footpaths through pastoral family farms, along rivers, and through gardens, and wildlife at nearly every turn. It was natural and perfect and so much of what I wasn't.

It was good for me to go because no matter how much I liked it there, I began to understand for the first time what home was. The homesickness I experienced was beyond missing family and friends. I was homesick for the farms and flat land and glimpses of defiant nature. The constant, underlying conflict that exists between hints of wildlife, developed crop land creating order and symmetry, farmers trying to persevere, great wealth and heart-breaking poverty literally next door to each other, the cultural diversities of the many people working and owning the land, small towns trying to keep their main streets unique while needing the revenue of housing developments all combine to give the place an energy difficult to define because it is so multi-faceted.

What began was the long, steady resolution with my own conflicts about this place. The pleasant childhood memories and the disdain, the desire to connect with nature and trying to find contentment in its fragments, the love of landscapes and coming to appreciate one that has been so altered, the growth, and the pollution in a home I now defend.

I returned, thankful that I had found a sense of place. And here I remain feeling, in one hand, sorrowful for those generations before me who kept moving, looking for their place to call home, hoping that with each move west they would find it, and grateful, in the other, for my parents' move.

ON A LATE spring day I set off north along Highway 99 and then west across 152, passing the tule elk refuges and water fowl sanctuaries near Los Banos, a last remnant of what this valley once was. I was headed for San Francisco to pick up my English friends flying over from London. This was the "Brits'" first trip to California, a father and mother with their daughter and her husband who were my age. As we descended the hills of Pacheco Pass, the valley came into view, a sight which still impresses me whether it is from the Sierra or the Ridge Route coming from Los Angeles. It was clearer that day than usual for the time of year. The expanse could almost be grasped, although the days of seeing both the Coast Range and Sierra in one encompassing spin are on most days now gone behind a gray sky. Once on the valley floor, the son-in-law, turned to me and said, "I don't believe I've ever seen so many shades of brown."

It is true the setting is the first characteristic someone internalizes about a region, before people, culture, or climate. I remember my first thoughts as I flew into Heathrow Airport in England to attend school. I had never before seen so much green.

We are a product of our region. I went to England, like most young people would do, to get a sense of who I was. What I learned was that I am where I come from. This valley and these farms, no matter how much I cursed them as a child, perhaps even because I felt this way, have made me, me.

I hear myself sound off in echo of my father, "this valley . . . ," and educate my English friends concerning its immensity. I go on to explain the terrain, not by any geological knowledge but by my eye. What I can't help but notice, living here all my knowing life. "Terrain?" they questioned, "it's flat!" In such a "flat" region one's eye picks up on the slightest rise, change of soil, or placement of crop. Cotton to the southwest, alfalfa north east of the Tulare Basin region, citrus within the folds of Sierra foothills, and where I live, in the eastern edge of the valley, grapes and fruit trees. The same area where, only two miles from my family's farm, the land rises and lowers with such abruptness it resembles a fault line. This fan dam land formation, known as the Sanjon de San Jose, was partly responsible for the formation of the Tulare Lake by keeping waters "down hill." And I let my British friends know that this spectrum of brown is in reality an irrigated desert, expansive and remarkable in its own right.

We each perceive beauty differently. The millions of city lights observed from London's St. Paul's Cathedral are extraordinary. But the single falling star seen from my back yard, which my British friends had never witnessed because of their city's night time glare, is more enchanting to me. I continue to look for the harmony in a landscape that has been transformed so dramatically from its natural self. The places of nature are now few and far between. From the edge of a scraped irrigation canal bank we notice an egret slowly walking. To observe it in its unaltered setting, we must stretch through barbed wire and look past a farmer's no trespassing sign and walk, if possible, the littered banks of the river.

More accessible is our current, man-made wilderness, a place where we now see nature abiding on new terms whether it is along a bare ditch bank or in the narrow rows of a vineyard. I have grown fond of my childhood memories. There is a reason why that recollection of re-planting our orchard when I was seven has remained so vivid. It is a moment of family and home and the connections to both.

18

And who hasn't leaned west, at least once? Caught
in the longing for something far off, over a hill,
around a bend—something just glimpsed in the
falling sunlight of evening and tinted gold. We are
each caught that way once or twice, struck dumb
by the possibility of a life altogether new.

—Sallie Tisdale,
Stepping Westward

TALKING WITH A distant cousin, we were trying to piece together the Apperson and Watts' seemingly coordinated moves in the Sierra Nevada and valley, the families criss-crossing paths prior to James Kimble and Elfleda's union in 1878 while still leaving large gaps in location and time. My cousin simply concluded, "Find the land, and you will find our family."

What is it that draws us to a place? I have often asked myself this while traveling down near desolate roads, only every so often spying a trailer or small shanty alone against the landscape. What makes us feel home and tells us we should stay? What made my ancestors travel from

Pennsylvania and Virginia to Missouri and Illinois, and then go on toward Oklahoma and Kansas, and finally to California? What was it that persuaded another side of my family to leave their homeland in Quebec and travel around Cape Horn to settle in northern California and, only a few years later, make the unsettled San Joaquin Valley their home? Why did my grandparents feel such a need to then leave this booming place to raise their children in the city, and why did my dad return?

I try to draw a common line between them all. For the most part, I am not left with the same answer twice. There were glints of gold, promise of cheap land, a better price for cattle, and in my case, a father who longed for the feel of the land and a sense of home. There are those that came for the land, for the love of working soil and the satisfaction of watching something grow—and not just their crops, but communities and families as well. All these ambitions brought me here to the place I will always call home.

I now realize I was raised with stories not just of family, as many people are, but also of landscape. The older I become, the easier it is to draw connections between the two. The land dictated how they built their lives whether it involved farming, mining, or commerce. These lives influenced each generation that followed. It is a rarity to be a fifth generation Californian. When I mention this fact to people, interested or not in the history of the valley or family, they act surprised. In states east it is not so uncommon to live in one place generation after generation, but so many Californians are newly transplanted. California is still the place of promise. I feel fortunate to have these accounts of journeys and dreams passed down to me through my family, to tie me here. I have likened this connection with the landscape to that of a newborn child where you want to do the impossible—the emotions so wrought-up—you want to engulf her presence, the heartache coming when she cannot reciprocate, when the sensation falls from expectations.

I still must embrace it. It is the beauty of resurgence and re-birth, not only seasonally but seen in the preservation of what lay before. It is family of past and future, and it has become stronger than I thought possible.

As I write this, I am due to give birth to my second child in a matter of weeks. Of course, I cannot help but wonder about the landscape he or his older sister will see in their lifetimes. Will it be more or less of pavement, family farms, preservation? What, if they decide to keep this region as their home, will they pass on to their children and grandchildren?

The other day a man with a camera drove onto my parents' farm, rang their doorbell, and asked if he could take pictures of their house and barn. "There's not a lot left like these," he said. He had his eight-year-old son with him. As my mother was telling me about this scene and the facts she relayed to this man about the history of the house and farm, I hoped his son was listening, listening to stories of the past, imagining for himself what those days were like and I wondered, if not now but someday, would he be concerned with the future of this place. And then I thought of my own children. I hope they too will listen, watch, and care as I have, and understand what it is to be connected to a place and know what it is to be home.

CREDIT

Wilma Elizabeth McDaniel's poem, "Self-Knowledge", first appeared in her chapbook collection of 35 poems entitled I Killed A Bee For You © 1987 by Wilma Elizabeth McDaniel published as the Vol. 34, No. 1 edition of The Blue Cloud Quarterly. All rights reserved © 2012 Back40 Publishing/ Stone Woman Press, Joshua Tree, CA.

BIBLIOGRAPHY

Audubon, John Woodhouse. *Audunbon's Western Journal 1849-1850.* Glorieta, NM: Rio Grande, 1969.

Barker, John. *San Joaquin Vignettes: The Reminiscences of Captain John Barker.* Ed. William H. Boyd and Glendon J. Rodgers. Bakersfield, CA: Kern County Historical Society, 1955.

Bolton, Herbert Eugene. *In the South San Joaquin Ahead of Garces.* Bakersfield, CA: Kern County Historical Society, 1935.

Boyd, William H. and Glendon J. Rodgers, eds. *San Joaquin Vignettes: The Reminiscences of Captain John Barker.* Bakersfield, California: Kern County Historical Society, 1955.

Brewer, William H. *Up and Down California in 1860-1864.* Ed. Francis P. Farquhar. Berkeley: U of California P, 1966.

Cleland, Robert Glass. *From Wilderness to Empire: A History of California.* Glenne S. Dumke, ed. New York: Knopf, 1959.

Cronise, Titus Fey. *The Natural Wealth of California.* San Francisco: Bancroft, 1868.

Fremont, John Charles. *The Exploring Expedition to the Rocky Mountains*. Washington, DC: Smithsonian Institution Press, 1988.

—. *Memoirs of My Life*. Chicago: Bedford, 1887.

—. *Narratives of Exploration and Adventure*. New York: Longmans, 1956.

Gist, Brooks D. *The Years Between*. Tulare, CA: Advance Register, 1952.

Gunsky, Frederic, R. ed. *South of Yosemite: Selected Writings of John Muir*. Berkeley: Wilderness, 1968.

Haslam, Gerald W. and James D. Houston, eds. "Origin of the Mountains." *California Heartland: Writing from the Great Central Valley*. Santa Barbara: Capra, 1978.

History of Tulare County, California. San Francisco: Elliot, 1883.

Holmes, Kenneth L. *Ewing Young, Master Trapper*. Portland, OR: Binfords, 1967.

Kaupke, Charles L. *Forty Years on Kings River 1917-1957*. Kings River Water Association, 1957.

Latta, Frank F. *Little Journeys in the San Joaquin*. N.p.: 1937.

Masumoto, David Mas. *Epitaph for a Peach*. San Francisco: Harper SanFrancisco, 1995.

Muir, John. *The Mountains of California*. Garden City, NY: Doubleday, 1961.

Norris, Frank. *The Octopus*. New York: Viking Penguin, 1986.

Platt, Suzy, ed. *Respectfully Quoted: A Dictionary of Quotations from the Library of Congress*. Washington, DC: Congressional Quarterly Inc., 1992.

Preston, William L. *Vanishing Landscapes: Land and Life in the Tulare Lake Basin*. Berkeley: U of California P, 1981.

Smith, Wallace. *Garden of the Sun*. Fresno, CA: A-1, 1939.

Stegner, Wallace. "A Sense of Place." *Where the Bluebird Sings to the Lemonade Springs*. New York: Penguin, 1992.

Steinbeck, John. *The Grapes of Wrath*. New York: Penguin, 1939.

Tisdale, Sallie. *Stepping Westward*. New York: Holt, 1991.

Uzes, Francois D. *Chaining the Land: A History of Surveying in California*. Sacramento: Landmark, 1977.

Valley Habitats: A Technical Guidance Series for Private Land. Managers in California's Central Valley. Ducks Unlimited. 14.2.

Yogi Stan, ed. *Highway 99: A Literary Journey through California's Great Central Valley*. Berkeley: Heyday, 1996.